AIFEST International Poetry Compilation
December 2020

Volume IV
Open Category

One Hundred Shades of Love
An Anthology of Love Poetry

**All India Forum for English Students, Scholars and Trainers
(AIFEST)**

One Hundred Shades of Love
An Anthology of Love Poetry

First Published
January 2021

Publisher
**All India Forum for English Students, Scholars and Trainers
(AIFEST)**

Copyright 2021 AIFEST

Amazon KDP ISBN: 9798585814907

Imprint
Independently Published

Editing and Proofreading
Manu Mangattu

About the Volume

To make optimum use of the Corona forced break from academic work, and to make learning fun, All India Forum for English Students, Scholars and Trainers (AIFEST) organized an Online International Poetry Competition for lovers of literature and poetry in November 2020. The participants were divided into three categories: Middle School (Classes V to VIII), High School (Classes IX to XII), and an Open Category for everyone else. Themes for poetry were different for different categories.

The results were announced on 20th November 2020, following which recitations of selected poems were compiled and posted on the Official YouTube Channel of AIFEST. We left no stone unturned to ensure free, fair and just evaluation and competition. We also made sure that unbiased and capable judges evaluated the poems. The relevant details were posted on the official blog and emailed to the participants. All the submissions were checked for plagiarism using both Turnitin and Urkund software.

Due to the huge volume of submissions we received, we had to omit many submissions based on the overall grade and score. We also understand that despite our best attempts, there could be subjectivity in evaluation and judgment. Pure objectivity, especially in evaluating poetry, is almost impossible.

From the Open Category, 252 poems were awarded A Grade. These were sorted and edited based on the subject matter, point of view, and treatment of the theme. This anthology features 100 A Grade winning poems handpicked by our editors on the theme 'Shades of Love'. It is sincerely hoped that this anthology will find its place in libraries and book houses as a periodical literary compilation documenting the output of a pandemic stricken multitude.

Poets Featuring in this Volume

1. Rima Bagchi, MA Student, Women's College, Bagbazar Kolkata, West Bengal
2. Shalini Majumdar, Newtown, Kolkata, West Bengal
3. Eusebia Kimde S Sangma, Bennett University, Greater Noida
4. S Saritha Sasidharan, Research Scholar, BITS Pilani Hyderabad Campus
5. Ardhra CS, Christ College, Irinjalakkuda
6. CG Akhila, MATS University, Raipur, Chhattisgarh
7. Hima Harry, Carmel College Mala, Thrissur, Kerala
8. Dr Amit Kumar Chandrana, Sri Ramsundar Sanskrit Vishwavidya Pratisthan, Bihar
9. Madhumathi H, Dargah Road, Zamin Pallavaram, Chennai
10. Lilit Anna Varghese, St Cyril's College, Adoor, Kerala
11. Payal Gupta, Peyarabagan Madhyamgram Kolkata
12. Namrah Rizvi, Karamat Husain Muslim Girls PG College, Lucknow
13. Haripriya Ravi, Karur, Tamil Nadu
14. Swetha M, SDNB Vaishnav College for Women Chengalpet
15. Sasmita Mishra, Bhubaneswar, Odisha
16. Joydeep Narayan Deb, Pragjyotish College, Bharalu Guwahati
17. Khushbu, Loyola Academy Degree & PG College Secunderabad, Telangana
18. Maria Alejandra Fumaroni, Buenos Aires, Argentina
19. Tuhina Roy, St Xavier's College, Fort, Thane
20. Meenakshi Yadav, Jawaharlal Nehru University, New Delhi
21. Anshu, University of Allahabad
22. Koyel Banerjee, Netaji Subhas Open University Bishnupur, WB
23. Dr M Marimuthu, Dr NGP Arts and Science College Coimbatore
24. Anakha Lakshmi NS, College of Applied Science Malampuzha, Palakkad

25. Debasri Debasmita Keshari, Krushnaprasad, Puri
26. Jeffrey Pauminlal @ Zester Frost, Churachandpur Manipur
27. M Sahila Nizar, Shermount College of Arts and Commerce, Erumely
28. Barasha Rani Saikia, Sibsagar College, Joysagar
29. Manvi Sharma, IGNOU, Maidan Garhi
30. Deepak Verma, Ex-Army Personnel, Lucknow, U P
31. Digant Trivedi, Vasai Road
32. Ankitha Raju, Mar Ivanios College, Thiruvananthapuram Kerala
33. Aardra AP, Mar Ivanios College, Nalanchira, Trivandrum
34. Dr Pallavi Bhardwaj, Kangra, Himachal Pradesh
35. Disha Pradeep Pawar, Masakalipalayam, Coimbatore
36. Azmi Azka Md Asif, GM Momin Women's College Thane
37. Greeshma Joseph, Jawaharlal Nehru University, New Delhi
38. Adegboye Adeyanju, University of Abuja-Nigeria
39. Athulya Lal, SFS College Nagpur
40. Dr AR Jyothi Priya, TSWRDC (W), Hyderabad
41. Thaamarai Selvi SP, Lady Doak College, Tallakulam, Madurai
42. Renita Dsouza, St John College, Palghar
43. Neena George Kunnath, Trivandrum International School, Kerala
44. Geethika KN, RMK Engineering College, Kavaraipettai Thirivallur
45. S Renuga Devi, VVV College for Women, Virudhunagar
46. Kaisar Mahmadiftikar Shekh, Anand
47. Madhavi Menon, Holy Cross Institute of Management and Technology, Calicut
48. Dr M Elangovan, Thiagarajar College, Madurai
49. Jayamurali, Sri Sankara Arts and Science College Kanchipuram, Tamilnadu
50. L Suriyakala, Sivagangai
51. Vishnupriya S, Kasturi College of Education
52. Nikunj Thaploo, Sector-15 Rohini, near Manav Chowk Delhi

53. Arundhuti Chakraborty, Calcutta University, Kolkata
54. Vipitha Devi, Paravur, Kollam, Kerala
55. Aswathi AS, Thrissur
56. Amit Pandey, Sidho Kanho Birsha University, Purulia
57. Kavya S Mony, Thiruvananthapuram
58. Debarpita Roy, Birati, Nazrul Path, Kolkata
59. Noor Fathima VN, MGAJ Arts and Science College N Paravur, Ernakulam, Kerala
60. Udatha Geetanjali, MMK & SDM College for Women Mysuru, Karnataka
61. Chetna Bhagoji, SKE'S Govindram Seksaria Science Degree College, Belagavi
62. Mohana A, K S Rangasamy College of Arts and Science Tiruchengode
63. RT Renikha Lettish, Holy Cross College, Nagercoil
64. Neena Paul, Anakkara
65. M Soni, Gudimalkapur, Hyderabad
66. Sagar B, DOSR in English, Tumkur University, Tumkur
67. Nzimiro Lazarus Ugo, University of Nigeria, Nsukka Enugu, Nigeria
68. Rounak Barman, The University Of Calcutta
69. Trayambika R N, MMK & SDM College for Women, Mysuru
70. S Arnisha Thangam, Holy Cross Home Science College Thoothukudi
71. M Saye Soozie, Annanagar, Chennai
72. Hridyesha Gogoi, Cotton University
73. Dhara Teraiya, Porbandar
74. Meenashy V, Shree Raghavendra Arts & Science College, Chidambaram
75. Sonali Sharma, Raipur Road, Dehradun, Uttarakhand
76. Dr Aparna Ajith, Assistant Professor in English at SNCW, Kollam
77. Srijana Subedi, Tribhuvan University, Central Department of Statistics, Nepal
78. Ranjitha Roy, Warsaw, Poland
79. Dr DR Pratima Roy, St Joseph's Jr Degree & PG College for Women, Kurnool
80. Pooja K Odedra, Rajivnagar, Porbandar

81. Sharanya H, Adi Sankara Training College, Kalady
82. Rasmi Menon, Ummanazhi, Palakkad, Kerala
83. Smita Kishore, NSCB PG College Lucknow
84. Bibu Binu Thomas, Pondicherry University, Kalapet Puducherry
85. Kapil Semwal, IGNOU, Uttarkashi
86. Krishangi Sarma, B Borooah College, Dr Bhubaneswar Guwahati, Assam
87. Anagha V, Mysuru Makala Kota & Shri Dharmasthala Girls College, Mysuru
88. Suji S, National Engineering College, KR Nagar Kovilpatti
89. Reena Joseph, St Ann's Degree College for Women Mallapur
90. Mary Jeniffer Samuel, Pondicherry University, Kalapet Puducherry
91. Shwetha RS, Lady Doak College, Tallakulam, Madurai
92. Sakshi Dubey, Amity University, Noida
93. Sonal Maharana, NES Ratnam College, Bhandup (W) Mumbai
94. Shehnaz Gujral, Salmiya, Kuwait
95. Ramsha Zaheen, Indira Gandhi National Open University, New Delhi
96. Punita, Rajpura, Jind, Haryana
97. Shweta Ghanshyam Punjabi, JG College of Commerce Ahmedabad
98. Sukrutha TS, Yuvakshetra institute of Management Studies Palakkad
99. Archana PV, University Campus, Calicut
100. Waheeda Bi Khan, Karnatak University PG Centre Kodibag, Karnataka

1
Do Love Last a Lifetime?

Rima Bagchi, MA Student, Women's College, Bagbazar
Kolkata, West Bengal

I privy to love.
My heart wanted something unique
Brain wanted perpetual.
Do love last a lifetime?
In answer, Life happened to me,
It made me a penchant for love.

I was seventeen, I first
Saw the charms of heaven,
A classmate, but unique in sense
Humorous yet chivalry at stake.
Approached me one day with a crude smile on face
It was no longer love; I sensed the fog.
He offered a night and took a look at my assets,
Oh! Poor Love,
You just became an old intertwined cassette.
A shade of love with lust at one pole
I just skipped and jumped to another whole.

Spring again hovered over my house
I came across my spouse.
He was thirty four I was twenty one
Many traced the odd but enquired none.
Thrill and adventure ran through my spine
I was eager to call him Mine.
A penchant for love as they say!

I was pleased with his appearance and sight
But my happiness could not see the daylight.
The bosom of romance was shattered at night,
He vigorously caught me under his might
Mother never taught me how to fight!
The 'love' continued every night
My might was dead and so was I.

My body was his only desire and crave,
Not me but he's now in grave.

"Widows don't love again"- society howled!
I shook and firmed at same.
I'm desirous and that's a fault
I'm ambitious and that's a fault.

I again fell for a man, younger than me
And full of thirst to quench.
I was a butterfly who needed her blossom
He moved with heart at sleeve.
All I wished for appeared into life,
Experience ceased and love made way
My body wanted warmth
He was the fireplace.
He was a Nomad,
I was a firefly who was free.
One day he was gone, as Nomads are known
"Ah! Unfortunate lady". No
Judgement was wrong. So I thought,
Love is not bound to force.
Let love free and acquire the moon
Be the bird and crib no soon.

Bonds and shades are prone to love
Love defines, hurts and shapes one.
Love is bliss, love is trauma, love is beautiful
Love is melancholy, Love is nothing
Yet it's everything.

I again wandered in the forest of Cupid
Met a man who was at his Autumn.
I was not Autumn but felt like one,
When he touched me I was in realms of fire.
I don't know if this will last,
But I'll never stop when I spot Love.
Different shades yet the flavour is same
All names are different yet Love is same.

2
Shades of Love
Shalini Majumdar, Newtown, Kolkata, West Bengal

I stared at your naked form with an intense gaze,
Clinging to you for solace and comfort, warmth and embrace.
Like a bawling babe to a mother's breast,
Or a young lover who seeks pleasure more than the rest.

I clasped your supple arms, drowning in heated pleasure,
Ignoring blatant reality, that love is both blithe and bitter.
It felt like spring anew, with blooming vitality, ecstasy and
charm,
To ease the pain of disgruntled kin who would only do me harm.

The reality was such: I, a man, and he the same too,
Intertwined our bodies to marvel at how quickly our love nest
grew.
The summer of our affair began with love, passion and a hope
for a lasting future,
Where the two of us could lay buried in limitless passion,
ravishing one another.

Steamy nights and sweltering days,
Wrapped in each other, we went blind and astray.
Folded laundry, bickered about politics and inclusivity,
Made passionate love without any care or adversity.

The flush of our romance, neither serious nor sombre,
Slowly turned into dull green and mellow ochre.
The summer of vibrance and vitality was slowly beginning to
fade,
The fall of our clandestine affair came not too late.

The streets were rough and barren,
Strewn with dead leaves and hollow goodbyes.
The air, cold and sullen,
A soft grey, with silent betrayals and unspoken lies.

Old wounds reopened, new ones made,
Lies, insecurities and false hopes raged.
"It's easy for you", he said, "you're out in the open."
"It's hard for me to admit to society and kin,
That all I do is lust for carnal sin."

'Carnal sin' you say? I wondered.
Is man inside man that ugly a thing?
Because a seed can't be planted,
Or birth a living thing?

The seeds of our love lay bare in the lifeless abyss of winter.
Gloom and doom filled the air,
What he uttered next only aggravated my disdain and despair.
"I can't do this anymore", he finally said,
"I have to live a 'normal' life, cure this 'disease' in my head."
"I have to marry a nice girl, put my kids to bed."

He ripped me apart, in mind and body,
Left, muttering empty words like goodbye and sorry.
The tears wouldn't flow; he had taken them all.
Dug my nails into my face: "Do you not care? Shriek and bawl!"

I drowned my sorrows in filthy sex and bitter drink,
Felt my body writhe in pain, shiver in agony, slouch and shrink.
What good was my body when all they wanted was a woman and
a babe,
Not love or fidelity, not even comfort in the shade.

Softly and steadily, came my respite.
Blue skies and peeping flower buds came into sight.
Spring held out his arms,
An earthly being in all its glory and charms.

His eyes shone clear and bright without cloud or mist,
A small tattoo of a sparkling rainbow flag gleamed on his dark
wrist.
With a springy skip in his step, he appeared
"Would you like to join our club?", he chirped.

"We share love and happiness, not fear or malice."

Those strong, dark arms, outstretched towards me,
Felt foreign yet friendly.
He said to me, "Treasure yourself before you seek it in others."
"What good is love and acceptance if your own sorry self
suffers?"
He who now wished to accept the society's 'abnormal' me,
Seemed like a love bundled in a pocket full of lilies.

3
Rainbow

Eusebia Kimde S Sangma, Bennett University, Greater Noida

Have you ever wondered
What is the Colour of love?
Is it red and pink;
Colours always mentioned in the same breath?
Or do you think it's black and blue
For love never comes without pain..
Love could be green, like the unyielding love of Nature
Or is the Colour of the sky just before the sun rises
Purple and orange- as if threatening a certain doom
It could be the colour yellow, for it reminds me of the rays of
sunshine greeting me through my window without fail
Perhaps, maybe, it is the colour white
Like how I assume a mother's love would be
So calm and pure.
All the colors culminated into one-
Pain, sorrow, suffering, peace, happiness and contentment
All rolled into one- Love.

4
My Irresistible Starlight

S Saritha Sasidharan, Research Scholar, BITS Pilani, Hyderabad Campus

Her feet danced softly along the snow-white floor,
As she made her way towards the black door.
The narrow corridors filled with light,
Could not compete with her vibrant vivacity - ever so bright.
She laughed and her eyes lit up with happiness,
She was pure innocence, without guile or falseness.
The lace shawl billowed around her like a wispy cloud,
As she smiled gently and turned her head half-around.
Silently she stretched her hand out,
Her gentle hand in mine dissolving all lingering doubt.
Her steps were firm and surefooted as she led me to the black door,
My being now entrusted to her evermore.

5
Shades of Love
Ardhra CS, Christ College, Irinjalakkuda

When the serene irony bowed
In front of a solitary hunter
Who belched love and moaned
In blackening pretentious love
Exquisite sunset blurred my eyes
With reddening curse of love.

It's a whorish bride who is void
Who once fell in the hands
Of a romantic loon
Who grasped her neck and kissed
With violence of motionless love

Love killed me with its blue ink
And drowned me in black
Now I'm floating dead in red

6
Some Shades of Love are Grey
CG Akhila, MATS University, Raipur, Chhattisgarh

Though you were dead for me,
the moment you raised your hands,
I still have kept you alive in me,
in some bits, parts, and strands.

Not as I love you anymore,
but to keep reminding myself,
how brave I was not to endure,
the ordeal and to escape that glass shelf,

where you would dump me back as a decorated doll,
showcasing and pretending as everything is alright,
after ruthlessly inflicting injuries on my body and soul,
and thrashing me the whole previous night.

I keep you alive,
to make me realize,
that how courageous
was I,
to rebuild my life
all over again,
knitting it's little broken pieces,
drenched in shades of pain.

As all shades of love,
may not be pink or gay,
some are sad,
and some shades of love are grey.

Though I wonder,
was it love at all,
as you always insisted,
and as they used to say.

**** (Dedicated to all the survivors of domestic violence.)****

7
My Comrade
Hima Harry, Carmel College Mala, Thrissur, Kerala

Friendship is a feeling
A feeling of Love
It amalgamates our hearts
It celebrates our precious moments
It satisfies our souls

Friendship is a feeling
A feeling of Love
It crafts our sense of compassion
It renovates our ideas
It promotes our pride

Friendship is a feeling
A feeling of Love
It strengths our tenacity
It appreciates our values.
It refines our bravery

Friendship is a feeling
A feeling of Love

2
It reflects our sense of faith
It inclines our deeds
It keeps our patience

Friendship is a feeling
A feeling of Love
It reveals our dreams
It weaves our wounds
It combines our virtues

Friendship is a feeling
A feeling of Love
It modifies our roles

It provides true wisdom
It grants serenity to identify the things

Friendship is a feeling
A feeling of Love
It rejoices in all our circumstances
It forgives our mistakes
It endures our misinterpretations

Friendship is a feeling
A feeling of Love
It convinces our optimism

3
It delights our performances
It assures in our sufferings

Friendship is a feeling
A feeling of Love
It boosts our ambitions
It makes us happy and healthy
It advocates a prosperous life

8
I Love You Mom
Dr Amit Kumar Chandrana, Sri Ramsundar Sanskrit
Vishwavidya Pratisthan, Bihar

The moment I opened my eyes,
In the kingdom of so called wise;
Bereft of ill-wills and ballyhoo!
For the very first time I experienced you.
I beckoned you mom but you didn't reply,
It was the moment my soul took a worthless fly.
It was the moment I missed you mom!
I love you mom, I love you.

Bathed in oil when I was compelled to barf,
Leaving me alone, you loved my scarf.
Almost alone I was just left to bawl,
And even nature left me helpless to make you a call.
Then creeping like a snail, I moved towards you,
But I found nobody there just to make me woo.
It was the moment, I missed you mom!
I love you mom, I love you.

After my breakfast when you handed over me
To my father and never returned to see,
How he baffled me with many acquaintances,
And never took any notice of my innocent utterances.
Ballsy, when I began to cry a lot,
He bashed me on my back and made that very hot.
Crying in pain, I missed you mom!
I love you mom, I love you.

Never had I learned a lesson as how to steal,
My friends taught me how to drill.
You always took the issue a light,
And warned me then when I took a height.
I repeated the truth before you many times
But you always kept me counting my crimes.
Losing my faith in truth, I missed you mom!

One Hundred Shades of Love

I love you mom, I love you.

When I grew a little, I still remember that fool
Who whispered something, I latter knew – school!
You beguiled me and threw me inside the gate,
Brusquing they dragged me inside, was that really my fate!
Beleaguered all the time, when I recalled you in my mind,
Not for a minute you spared me a glimpse or waited behind.
Making myself belligerent, I missed you mom!
I love you mom, I love you.

Later I inured myself, just for your sake
But love and touch became words quite fake.
Mom, you asked me why I was turning so lurid,
I will answer you that if you really need.
That day I remember well, you called me a collegiate,
Your love – your kisses, you left for me no gate.
It was the moment I missed you mom!
I love you mom, I love you.

Then I turned an intrepid son of a maudlin mother
And you too began to treat me like the other!
My physical nature kept me aloof of my thoughts,
It was the time you had taught me what was what.
For all your mistakes, I but kiss your crown,
Now I know why you are called mom.
It's the moment I miss you mom!
I love you mom, I love you.

On this earth you created a man out of an inane,
You're the life giving agent if I was an insane.
Mom, come once more, see your son, commit a big mistake,
Take me out of this hell, without you I, too, am fake.
Love your kingdom, love your life, love you mom – forever,
Your love is here, your love is there; now it's time to gather.
This is the moment I miss you mom!
I love you mom, I love you.

9

The Palette Speaks

Madhumathi H, Dargah Road, Zamin Pallavaram, Chennai

The browns of the Earth!
In its invisible layers
He hid his words
Like rain, as love lashes upon his heart
Honey-soaked whispers exude
Petrichor-scented words sprout
In lush green, upon her barren soul
Bronze canvas and, emerald art
Near yet far...
Where will she hide the colour
That blooms as she blushes
When the Earth turns her
Into a forest of flowers...
Who will stop the wind, from
Carrying the fragrances of every petal
Gossiping about her love...
And
Who will stop her, from buying pitchers
For mirages, and
Stop him - the Earth, from drinking her tears
With an unquenchable thirst...
Oh the myriad shades of love
Pleasure and pain, painted upon the canvas of life
Unpredictable tears, and laughter
Smiles, and frowns the shades leave behind...
In Mysterious blue of the night, enigmatic purple
The unspoken words blanket her as quilts
On colder winter nights
Her eyes longing for the bonfire of happiness
Warm flames blooming as yellow, orange petals...
Under the milky blue Sky
Shade of vast unbound wings, hope sprouts...
In the color of rain, love gently showers upon her soul
Silvery, shimmering strings and drops
Like tapestry and sequins...

Kisses planted in dreams, are embroidered as poems
Multi-colored designs wink at her
Each shade of love, carry a story
Warm, cool, soft...each color's voice
Speak the language of love
Bold, chirpy, shy, however love speaks
It is love that anchors the soul
It is love that shoulders the world
She, he, you or me
It isn't the shade of love that matters, but
Its colourfastness, that makes life
A timeless artwork of love...

10
Soggy Dream
Lilit Anna Varghese, St Cyril's College, Adoor, Kerala

She welcomes the proximity of his coming
he incarnate his appearance to her
broken all the laws of heaven to his beloved
he gently touch her
suddenly change her attitude to
coarse of rock became cobble
cobweb became wrinkle
they deeply bound with love
and colour their dreams
the drop of rain get deep into her mind
each drop sounds the depth of their love
suddenly,
gust of wind came
she fall asleep
he disappear
she fall a drowse, to drowsy
a soggy dream.
Dawn appear again
daffodil glisten
in glen.
But here her soul,
wait for the sound of his love.

11
To The Heart's End
Payal Gupta, Peyarabagan Madhyamgram Kolkata

The ripples that stirred love,
Died as a regenerating dove.
The takeaway is a preferable outlook,
Which denied a solace barefoot.

Inexperience pleased a sour of constant
Experience forbade sparkles, heart and heart beats.
The skipped steps to the throne;
In sweet, salt, pungent and erect,
had bent itself far from recognition.

The autumn approaches uninvited, with winter permanent.
The significant spring failed its magnificence in summer.
To an undefined child, the blessing of the wild,
To a societal child, the blessing of the mild
is malicious, treacherous and vile.

Walking into the grey, searching of dark,
The light faithfully waited for access.

The figure of maternal affection is endless.

Destructive shadows always fetched a hand,
Promised a forever, and existed never, but
Always made a better ever.

The shade wilfully sheltered us,
When 'I' and 'You' are distant truce.
The bloom once cherished tranquillity, is now a disturbed ability
'He' loved, 'She' loved, 'They' never loved.

Is 'together' important? Is 'happily ever after' important?
Importance was of the bubble, which destroyed reality.
A broken land is so graceful to understand the fall.
The cracked pieces survive to break or make again.

Healing isn't the overture to the core,
The untouched faith is journeying towards best,
The silent road is the way to a defensive decay.

Motions into emotions are fragile, yet agile
in wait, process and end.

12
Unconditional Love

Namrah Rizvi, Karamat Husain Muslim Girls PG College
Lucknow

If I get another life..
I promise I will spend that;
Standing under your shades and
Sitting upon your roots..

But in this one
I have a family behind
Whom I promised that I will come back soon..
I assured them
That
This journey will be full of boon.

But oh you my friend..
Yes you..
I have to leave you for this life..
And go upon my goals..
But you teach me a lot..

That how to be strong, steady and
Always live for others..
I am thankful
And always remember that how u cooled
My summers..

13
You and Me
Haripriya Ravi, Karur, Tamil Nadu

When trinity of "You" is added with twain "Me", it
automatically results in complete
"We".
Where,
"We" is the synonym of "Woo" and
Antonym of "Woe".

14
Shades of Love

Swetha M, SDNB Vaishnav College for Women, Chengalpet

Caring brings me and you close
Memories and moments with selfie pose
Lots of possessiveness takes a start
Lovely secrets to share with you
And I will always stay to say I love you
Expectations hurt, but small gifts and surprise
To see the way your face with grace
Promises that engraves your emotion
Fights and problems are caution
Always and forever you and I
Whatever happens, just do or die
Statements and situations gives a lesson
I made love badly and still finding the reason!

15
Love
Sasmita Mishra, Bhubaneswar, Odisha

Love, Love, Love -
It is the precious gift of God,
Love is life;
The care of a mother for her child
is the epitome of love one can find.

Love is divine, pious and eternal -
Lord Krishna and Radha made it immortal,
Times to come and times to go,
but their divine love will be there forever.
Love is a rainbow, full of colours,
It's like the deep rosy petals,
It's the first dew falling on the winter grass.
It begins with the story between Adam and Eve,
It will be there forever till the end of humanity.

Love is the only language understood by all.
It starts from within and pervades everywhere,
From a tiny insect to a gigantic creature of this Earth-
Love is penance, love is salvation,
Love is commitment-
the subtly sung hymn of creation.
Sans love, life is bleak like a monotonous monologue,
Love enriched life shines, like two love birds twitted dialogue.

16
Naoko

Joydeep Narayan Deb, Pragjyotish College, Bharalu, Guwahati

Dear Naoko,
Every night I served you haiku
And ignored your bruises
I thought that was a part of your make up.

As I undressed your kimono,
You looked like a Japanese Sakura,
Branches crawling out of hands
Fingers turning into twigs
Your hair, eyebrows, lips and
Breasts metamorphosed into flowers
Roots wrapping your knees
Not letting you to leave
This place, this marriage or this man.

In late March or early April
When Sakura blossom,
You weep in the kitchen
You sob in the bathtub
You don't smile for three weeks.
They blossom, You don't.
I don't let You blossom.

I exploit my bonsai Sakura
Like I exploit you,
Every night in bed
You died out of thirst
Just like my tree.
But this time,
As I undressed your Kimono
You looked like my bonsai
Which died three days ago.

17
Your Mistake but I'm Sorry
Khushbu, Loyola Academy Degree & PG College
Secunderabad, Telangana

*(They play victim but we say sorry because we can't see them
going, even though they're wrong. How self-love and esteem
loses itself, in front of the love for them.)*

People to people these mindsets vary,
How much of sadness will this heart carry?
Let me be the one and say you sorry,
Because nothing's the same as it was before,
Life has changed on a complete whole,
And I'm standing here all alone.
I wish you were by my side,
But we are a million miles aside.
Not through distance but as the feelings flow,
You never came back but still remember, I know,
You and I; being us with that glow, you know.
Sorry again! 'cause my words would be soar,
But they are true, I could have sworn!

The shadow itself has covered me all,
This mystery of finding us, will never be solved,
'Cause 'someone' made people involved,
Or else things would have been resolved.
Darkness or lights, I was still okay with our fights,
At least we could share or complain and we had
some fear of losing each other, right?
Well, I saw my future with you; so bright
That I tried with all my might,
But couldn't bring you back to our hive,
Sorry to bother you now but I'm still half alive.
I am so low that I am really high,
Sober so far, need myself to face me but I sigh.

You are in my heart and you'll always be there,
Let the things change or shatter here and there.

Now no one's going to speak because you don't care.
We wouldn't have been apart but you....
We were always for each other; but you
You always wanted a different path, without me,
Without us and yet again you chose it here too.

I still remember everything, just like our small fights over that
chocolate mousse.
But all you had to say was, "I'm done with you!"
I don't understand how you moved on so fast,
Like there was nothing between us in our past,
Because I'm still standing here, where you left me alone and
moved on,
My heart cannot forget it's other half because those memories are
forever with me
and only you moved on.

I give you all my happiness because you were all I had and take
all your pain,
Maybe by this there's something or some part of you that I will
still regain.
I'm trying to stay alone in my pain but your memories won't
leave me again,
Oh I am Sorry again!

18
The Right Place
Maria Alejandra Fumaroni, Buenos Aires, Argentina

Life is always welcome, a new birth has almost appeared.
Cold but not humid, nobody at home, only us three.
It has had lunch before, not far away from here.
Delicious, new tasties, smelling, laughing, memories.

Cold but not humid, nobody at home, only us three.
Full of happiness is nothing compared with that.
Delicious, new tasties, smelling, laughing, memories.
Some bread with tea to celebrate, sometimes fear comes to us
and knocks on the door.

Full of happiness is nothing compared with that.
Don´t push the door, go away.
Some bread with tea to celebrate, sometimes fear comes to us
and knocks on the door.
It could be the right place but it couldn´t.

Don´t push the door, go away.
I would be more than happy that everything happened there, at
least started there.
It could be the right place but it couldn´t.
Change didn't appear, the mood flipped all day long.

I would be more than happy that everything happened there, at
least started there.
Sunshine over the moon, sunset who knows.
Change didn't appear, the mood flipped all day long.
If I had planted my root beside you?

Many paths to be walked are there waiting anxiously for us.
It has had lunch before, not far away from here.
Hold my hand and look at both sides.
Life is always welcome, a new birth has almost appeared.

19
Untitled
Tuhina Roy, St Xavier's College, Fort, Thane

in the end of this story i wish to recreate
to tell that it'll be different this time,
the sky will be red and not blue
and there'll be more wilderness than true;

it leaves me wanting more than ever;
i scurry away, dissatisfied and heavier
not wishing to end this here,
cuz in the end of this story i wish to recreate

let it be yrots or otsry, anything but linear
and not what it was supposed to be;
perhaps unpredictability is a joy,
cuz in the end of this story i wish to recreate

dreams are free, it always was and will be,
let them be seen, by every being--
burn the flesh with passion and castastrophe
cuz in the end of this story i wish to recreate.

tranquility is for the child-like, we're not-
our dreams are strange and filled in chaos,
never to be touched, like it's to be numbed

cuz in the end of this story i just wish to recreate.

20
The Throes
Meenakshi Yadav, Jawaharlal Nehru University, New Delhi

Person: hi.
Me: hi!
Person: how are you?
Me: I am...
[Struggling mostly.
Trying hard and failing miserably.
The script seems amiss and I feel confused really.
There is an intense urge,
a desire,
a longing,
almost like a compulsion.
It feels like I am journeying from intense pain,
to more pain,
to an understanding,
to a mind over matter situation,
to numbness.
I am seeking transcendence but reaching only numbness.
I have been telling others some lies
and I have been telling myself some truths.
I feel if this world was a better place I would be dancing right
now.
I feel I need to adjust my attitude and play my hand.
I feel I know exactly how to save myself from all this trouble,
and yet,
here I am in my own personal portable hell.]
... I am great!

21
Adhokshaja
Anshu, University of Allahabad

Is this but my illusion?
Your pale *peetaambar*?
Your eyes studying mine?
Non-existent you seem!

Is this but my dejection?
Your sudden coming to me!
Your unannounced departure!
Your invincible being.

Is this but my surrender?
You're everywhere I breathe!
I lay my flowers at your feet,
You lead me to infinite.

[1]*Adhokshaja – One who is beyond knowledge acquired through senses. Another name of Lord Krishna.*
[2]*Peetaambar – Yellow garments. Worn by Krishna.*

22
Love

Koyel Banerjee, Netaji Subhas Open University, Bishnupur, WB

Once, When I had no sleep in my eyes,
I was in a lot of trouble and Life seemed so unnecessary to me;
Suddenly YOU came and we became best friends,
YOU are the one to whom I don't hesitate to share my feelings,
Even though I talk over stupid things, YOU just listen and say
My voice is beautiful;
When I feel low YOU make me smile,
Even though YOU feel sleepy, but YOU stay awake for me;
YOU take my all troubles as yours and YOU give the reason to
make my life fruitful.
After My Parents, YOU are the one who takes care for me more
than anybody;
YOU make me realize What is the LOVE actually.

23
The Dream of Orpheus

Dr M Marimuthu, Dr NGP Arts and Science College
Coimbatore

Fate indulged the game of life,
Leaving aloofness upon me,
And extirpating the grain of hope.

The soul yearned for eternal love,
Conferring salvation upon me,
And relieving from the infernal life.

Suddenly I had the sight of an archangel,
Like fireflies twinkling the oval eyes,
And whispering with a feeble voice.

The melody filling the mind with bliss,
Melted the pangs in the heart,
And deposited me into the world of love.

Oh my love! Offering joyful pain,
Expelled the dilemma within me,
And abruptly vanished in the dawn.

24
Triumph of Love
Anakha Lakshmi NS, College of Applied Science, Malampuzha
Palakkad

They were disunited by a new life!
But the world endeavoured
To bring them together!
Took them to the same corners,
Through the same paths.
But enthralled by the adventures
They never found each other!
Time waylaid
To part them.
They wandered through all the paths,
Not knowing
They were in the same path.
Fortunately the World won,
As their souls connected
At the first glimpse.
But time still kept them apart!
Their life being a mystery,
They were flustered,
"we shouldn't have met"!
Like the moon that comes back
To visit the world every night,
They came back to each other,
Every time they part.
Conceding that they could never part.

Love wasn't something
that time could conquer !
Even time had to bowe in front of it
Because love is what unites the world!

25
Shades of Love
Debasri Debasmita Keshari, Krushnaprasad, Puri

Once you were my sunshine,
Dusk, dawn, fog and rain;
As forever comes never
I was left alone in the pain.

Forgot about love, lust and lost
Loved persistently like amaranthine;
But I was shattered into pieces
Became maimed, cracking my own spine.

Then I stifled a cry alone
Knew a new tinge of love,
How you shoved me out of your life
Into the hell and hollow.

Your inclination, insinuation on can't calculate
The warmth and depth of my love;
What I considered to be the shade of love
Is actually a Crater, perhaps my grave.

Still feeling confined, captivated by your heart
My eyes yearn for a glimpse of you,
There is no love yet love is there
Is this the real shade that lasts forever and ever...??

So.....
I have to lose myself to make myself win
To light up this darkness which I discover,
Now no need to fret my dear
I know everything is fair in love and war....

26
Shades of Love
Jeffrey Pauminlal @Zester Frost, Churachandpur, Manipur

Love is not an emotion,
Tossed around like the waves of an ocean.
It's a choice of the will,
To care and sacrifice even through life's downhill.

Love birds meet and fly away,
But some drift apart even on the same day.
When the warm fuzzy feeling is gone,
They think that love had moved-on.

No. Just like how our parents,
Showed us love along with our closest friends.
Love is a sacrifice for someone,
Never saying the words "I'm done!".

But the Love greatest above them all,
Is the Love of Jesus Christ for our heavenly call.
The Son of God who died for sinners like us,
While we were enemies with a dreadful past.

The love of Christ is like the sun,
That gives life and is the one.
The love of families is like the moon,
That illuminates the night with a soothing tune.

But the Love of our lovers,
Is like the star,
That stayed closest to the moon,
And never wanders off far.

All shades of love has no point of reference,
Without the love of Christ that has no end.
To eternity and beyond it will never fade,
And teaches us how to nurture, sacrifice and to aid.

27
Shades of Love
M Sahila Nizar, Shermount College, Erumely

Every time a shadow came close to me
I too melted into that shadow.
Whenever he lay in the darkness
You are with me as a shadow.
The way I went, followed me
Also included as a safety net....

Whenever I sit still in grief
You opened the shield of love.
Every time I was in your memories
He gave me the key to life.
When I look into the distance
I miss you…
Yet in this world
You become just a shadow.

Whenever I want to see you
You came to my side like my shadow.
In the light of the candle
You protected me like a light.
You shade color to my life.
Still, can't show you.
Your real form of beauty.

I want to see it.
Please, show your real form of beauty
Because, I love you…
My precious heart is waiting for you
Please come to me close.
I want to see you dear
Then only; my life be shaded with colors.
I don't know how to see?
But, I know, still I really love you
It's the real love.
Real love for ever seen in this world.

28
Sprouting Heart
Barasha Rani Saikia, Sibsagar College, Joysagar

Allotting her a little time
She writes a fraction in his name.

Furnishing tear she keeps the plants alive
No rain comes.

She knows nothing regards him
Without knowing name he is a precious stone.
Recognising his popularity by machinery
She understands she has no right to make him own.

He is a man of love
He is a man of work
He is a man of society

Love is art,
Hope is alive;
One day,
He will come.
The last leaf of her life plant
Will not drop down.

29
Blindfold
Manvi Sharma, IGNOU, Maidan Garhi

Between those layers of skin
I found you like the rainbow in the sky
Deceptive of its nature,
You made me look closer to your lies.
Magic, glitter, hope and lies
You brought all after the storm had arrived.
To some, it is not visible
And as some find it unreasonable
I, on the palette of life,
Synchronized our hue,
And the sky turned purple
Framing it as our cue.
In the space on time
When the stories were created,
We always found a room for celebrating
With a pinch of grey in it.
Love, pride, serenity
Tokens of serendipity,
All was lost when as night crawled in
Splashing the darkness on the screen.
Calling upon the night,
I called the devils
After the sun was set
I lost you as the rainbow left.
The colour of my soul
Lost its meaning
When I lost my existence
In the black world of dullness.
The dullness that fades shine of the colour
Every colour that is vibrant and sharp
Reflecting my inner self,
I wanted to glow.
Tying up all my colours
I wanted to save myself,
But I am drowning in the lake

Of the black land.
Looking at the colours again,
My body - that is pink, blue and green
Gathers all the black
That resides in me
Making me a part of their black world again.
Our moments that I kept beside my heart,
Did no longer any good to me
As the demons of the memories were crawling up within me
Scratching down every ounce of my skin
Similar to the touch of my prince
I was mesmerized with so much of love within me
Which was not had to happen with the demons
But for the man I was with!
Waiting, hoping, astonished
I found myself in cries again,
For one storm has passed away
To magnify another rainbow next morning.

30
Love: A Mystery
Deepak Verma, Ex-Army Personnel, Lucknow, UP

The most beautiful blessings of Almighty-
Bestowed upon human beings.
Can be defined not; but felt merely.
Plays the foremost role in life surely.
Dwells everywhere; knows no boundaries;
Possessed by all.
A necessity- to some, a treasure- to many.
The best enjoyed stuff- A thing of beauty.
What am I?
I am nothing but, **LOVE**!
Yes! I am love; without which,
No existence of the universe can be expected.
I am the only, that is unconditional and non-judgemental.
I do not always have to be an outward projection.
But something, that exists and must be exercised internally.
Yes! I am Love.
Several people have defined me in several ways.
In someone's perception, I have been exposed as-
Love encompasses infinite shades.
On exploring the brighter face of the love;
One perceives that-
Love is inevitable; love is eternal.
Love is incredible; love is beauty.
Love is ecstasy; love is sacrifice.
Love is omnipotent; love is omnipresent.
Love is soul; love is divine.
Love is prayer; love is worship.
Love is manic; love is salvation.
Love is voyage to heaven;
Love is something-
That completes; that touches.
That enwraps; that engulfs.
That pleases; that unites.
That heals; that decorates.
That conjugates; that embraces.

That tickles; that whispers.
That teases; that buoys.
That provokes; that binds.
That does not discriminate.
That can never be pilfered.
That can never be avoided.
That induces immense pleasure,
Aiming at survival.
That shows the path;
That supersedes everything.
By winning over everything.
But, costs nothing.
But eh! it is **Mysterious.**
Yes! love is a mystery; could not be solved;
Rather, should be enjoyed.
That never dies' and leads to redemption.
Thus, love is everything.
But, on exploring the darker face of the love;
It manifests different perception; that-
It is disguise who wears a magical cloak.
Which, reveals that-
It breaks; it kills.
It spoils; it deprives.
It destroys; it hurts.
It is horrible; it is painful.
That leads to damnation.
Eventually- love is everything.
It compels a true lover to invoke Almighty.
And, urge to arrive and enwrap the lover in his magical cloak;
Lest, Almighty should loses his own- the most precious jewel
(lover);
The way lover himself has lost his most lamented gem.
Yes! love is a riddle; which can not be solved.
Hence, one must dive into the mystery of love.
And, loses its virginity.

31
New Flower
Digant Trivedi, Vasai Road

An older self, I was consumed,
The remnants of which, I exhumed,
From a rickety, dark drawer,
From a younger phase, I saw her.

But nary a fleeting feeling,
Only indifference in me, reeling,
I felt like a cold dry stone,
Round, and lying alone.

Beaten to shape by the flow,
And heated in the sun's glow,
I now found a new shore,
And life became much more.

The older self was dead,
A new path now lay ahead,
Sail with the winds, higher,
I lit my old self on fire.

The ashes fertilize the soil,
Of new love's labour and toil,
For through this love and power,
Will blossom my new life's flower.

32
Crepuscule
Ankitha Raju, Mar Ivanios College, Thiruvananthapuram, Kerala

The cloudy sky brings an unparalleled beauty with it,
Turning my blues and greys,
Into an unknown amethyst and purpureus,
Turning the dichromatic lone sky,
Into a prismatic space.

The twilight shades that we paint on each other,
The mauve, the lilac,
The lavender and the fairy tale,
Will they remain pristine?

The me that you give me,
And the you that I gift you,
Will they remain the same?
Will our shades fade away from each other?

The sun takes you away with him,
A thousand miles away from me,
Leaving me alone with his moon,
Who changes her shape every day,
Hoping to patch up my broken pieces by herself.

The purple tint that you leave,
It makes me want to stay.
The smeared pink streaks,
They make me want to breathe.
The scarlet,
Steals from me all of you,
And paints it on the rosy sky.

The wait from the very dawn,
Unbearable without you.
Your arrival,
Your presence,
Pulls me out from this unknown dark.

You seem different elsewhere,
So, I long to be always home,
For you're perpetually there for me, there.

33
Paradise of Love
Aardra AP, Mar Ivanios College, Nalanchira, Trivandrum

Two loving hearts
Sparing those peaceful sleeps
To Be by my side
In my breathless nights

A huge chest to rest my head,
Hands that provide me everything
Ignoring his burning Pocket,
Always by my side
Despite being weak,
To instill words of courage,
Is my Dad.

A weak weary arms,
To warm my ice cold fingers,
Evade away my fears,
With long pampering hugs,
She, My mom
Fills my Tummy with sweet Aroma.

Having them near,
A Paradise on Hell!
What more you need
Than this selfless care?
What else is bliss
Than their chanting prayers?
How lucky is a soul
To feel the Divine through them?

34
Soulmate (Dedicated to the Unborn Child)
Dr Pallavi Bhardwaj, Kangra, Himachal Pradesh

Potential to respire within an immure edifice,
The beauteous existence with a cord makes thou a bliss.
Thine is me and I am you,
The state of adoration is in rapport too.
Listening to the petit beats of a soul,
Has become the being's apex goal.
Breathing in concord seems enlightening,
Round the clock your thoughts make me rising.
Desperately waiting for the joyous fraction,
When thy'll be in my arms with a euphoric elation.
Grasping a yearn within for so long,
Has taken a shape which will undoubtedly, be greeted by a
throng.
Come … Rise … Utter … Laugh …,
Fill my being hood with a superlative swap …

35
A Reverie in Spring
Disha Pradeep Pawar, Masakalipalayam, Coimbatore

Everything around me looks like snowy dove,
Seems like there's no heaven above,
Yes, I am in Love...

Days passed until I realized how I felt,
The heart inside me had begun to melt;
I could not help but dream,
For, my world revolved around him.

I visualized the new me,
Completely dressed, pretty to see;
I could see myself go crazy,
Just like the springs with a daisy.

Isn't it lovely,
How he occupied me totally;
How his smile made me smile easily,
I guess he liked me too secretly.

36
Ancestral Beliefs
Azmi Azka Md Asif, GM Momin Women's College, Thane

She still believes in what the ancestors speak,
Still she used to sit in the front yard every night,
With aching heart and brawny love,
Staring up in the sky,
Searching for the moon and stars,
Sometimes she blushes,
Sometimes she whimpers,
With the desire,
Whether he also peers for her in late night
And who knows,
He does.

37
The Silhouette
Greeshma Joseph, Jawaharlal Nehru University, New Delhi

I used to be a silhouette,
Waiting for a rainbow to hue.
The tints were satisfiable and yet they went away,
Took my shade with them.
I remained pale under the shadow of memories.
I waited for a rain so beautiful soon.
It came though;
This time there were more tones,
But yet they went away,
Took my shade with them;
And this persisted.
But I no longer remained a portrait.

38
IF
Adegboye Adeyanju, University of Abuja-Nigeria

If hearts are books
Chapter upon chapter
Page by page
Line by line
Each word would have been exhaustively read
Interpreted and analysed…

If hearts are physicalized structures
Inch by inch each element would have been gleaned:
Blocks, cement, sand, stone and nails
Water even and sweat and all
Prints of masons and carpenters
And painter's brush strokes betrayed
And electrician's fraudulent wiring detected

If you're painstaking and patient yet
All that seems a mystery would become a revelation clear
Clearer than spring unpolluted and fresh

If words were adequate
If feelings could express
If writing would do the trick
Page by page
Letter by letter
You'd plead I stop trying to try!
Alas! You still don't know that you know

If only you know that you now
Or rather acknowledge that you know
You drive me away and into the arms of another

If only that you know
I'm not one to violate you
If you know---If you know
Or if you know?

39
A Dilemma
Athulya Lal, SFS College Nagpur

All my emotions cluster
when I think of the word LOVE.
It must be the only feeling that's combined
of all possible emotions in the world.
Some say love is beautiful,
some say it's scary.
I say it's a beautiful dilemma

On one hand it proves the existence of the humanity,
on the other, It can cause the end of it.
Some express the love through their beautiful arts,
Some prove it by destroying the mankind.
Yes, Love is a dilemma.

It makes you feel secure,
It gives you a reason to smile,
It gives you a ray of hope,
It gives you a reason to live your life.
But also, It gives birth to insecurities,
It's the reason you cry,
It can make you despair,
It might erase your will to be alive.
Remember, love Is a dilemma.

It's a mother's unconditional care for her wean,
who protects it from all the evil of this sphere.
It's also the rage in that lover's eye,
which destroyed kingdoms for the Love he was denied.
It's the reason of your determination,
it's the reason of your depression.
It's the reason you preserve those old pictures,
but, it's also the reason you pluck that radiant flower.
As I said, Love is a beautiful dilemma.

Love is that big decorated cage

with everything two birds need,
you got your life secured and a life companion to meet
but you lack the freedom to fly over the mountains and seas.
Whereas, if you are freed,
it's hard to say if you would find food, a partner
or if you would even live for a week.
SO, we all stay in this bubble of dilemma
cause our existence is acknowledged here
and our lives have bigger reason to sustain.
Love is a dilemma, which no one can escape.

40
How Shall I Tell
Dr AR Jyothi Priya, TSWRDC (W), Hyderabad

How shall I tell
the world I love thee
Not the way one would think I love
but the way the words just can't *tell*
I remember
the smell of brown wet earth
and wafting hot coffee ladled in our hands
our long talks
sitting by the balcony overlooking deep blues

How shall I tell
the world I love thee
Not the way one would think
but the way the words just cant *tell*
Time has passed. You were a Golden heart my dear!
You are my eyes, what not!
I want to hold your hand my dear
You radiate strength and a smile I can't forget
I see me in you, every time!
Yet our births were not alike
Nor are the markers we wear everywhere
As indicators of our distinct race and religion
Love is sans these borders of division
I see stars at night twinkling for us at us;
Well, whats wrong in dreaming anyway?
The stars don't lie, dazzling darling stars!!
They would be with us
Twinkling together just like us
Come what may!

How shall I tell
The world I love thee
Not the way one would think I love
But the way the words just can't *tell*
Hark! I will love thee even in inaction!

41
Shades of Love

Thaamarai Selvi SP, Lady Doak College, Tallakulam, Madurai

When wisdom drives her,
with the craze to seek the unseen pages of life,
through the wildness of storm,
you're beside her;
proving education is just a part,
whereas filled with values and compassion
matters the most.
you walk into her life;
like the drops of rain on a drought land.
you often say her, "to change one's life for good,
be ready to face the world."
She's blessed for this unconditional love,
which drives the essence of eternity.
whenever the fear of losing,
squeezes her heart,
your words of hope,
cycles round her body to and fro,
roots the spirit of fortitude
by nourishing love.
It's still a wonder,
nothing in life is precious
when she gives you,
the artistry of granting
drops of tears with smile together,
like sunshine mixed with rain;
when she has changed her
signature to autograph.
To All the Artists of My Life.

42
Shades of Love
Renita Dsouza, St John College, Palghar

That what is boundless and within,
Rests inside an inn,
Unconditional, seamless and true,
Pure, soulful you,
That what abounds in care,
To all equal, never unfair,
Love! Divine so deep,
Love! Majestic, a faith leap,
Love so sacred of thine,
Love unchanged with time,
Connecting the receiver and giver,
Love is an ever-flowing river,
It knows not to receive,
But flows only to give,
It is clear inside out,
And content with or without,
It transpires every hardship,
And strengthens every friendship,
A gift by God to all,
An emotion not so small,
Deeply felt inside,
Of which nobody can hide,
Numerous are the shades of love,
But to each it must smile and serve,
Surprising as it may seem,
Love can both save and redeem,
It is a connecting cord,
A cord connected to God,
A connection to be felt,
An emotion to be dealt,
Something.......
that binds,
And yet liberates!!

43
My Oath of Baldness for Love
Neena George Kunnath, Trivandrum International School Kerala

Why do I rouse up in my slumber?
Only to find myself in the solace of darkness...

Why do I wait in my chamber?
Only to remind myself that I am forbidden of my far away fille
princess...

Why do you haunt my memories to make me so forlorn?
O merciless materfamilias of my nativity...

Why do you dastardly deny of ma rights in entirety?
Only if I could embrace a stroke of serendipity...

Why will I not embosom her till eternity?
O ye peep! Mark my words of unruliness...

Why would I remain a pantaloon hairless and careless?
Only until my rendezvous with my progeny...

Why would you relate my bare baldness to bogging boldness?
Only that I simply do not care of your misogyny.

44

Iris of my Felicity

Geethika KN, RMK Engineering College, Kavaraipettai
Thirivallur

Found something new and crystal,
me being a wanderer around the land,
Launching me from my pistol

Saw the dirt on your cheek, but ironical
your heart, gold dust all my hand.
Found something new and crystal

You took me off the skeptical
hook, causing me to dive in the sand.
Launching me from my pistol

Go places with you and sunny, festal
days to remember how our skin got tanned.
Found something new and crystal

So cold, pulled the cover up, now my total
feet are out, saw him covering'em, through a strand.
Launching me from my pistol

Just woke up next to you and felt magical
Up in the skies, far from the woolly stand.
Found something new and crystal
Launching me from my pistol.

45
True Love is Worth the Wait

S Renuga Devi, VVV College for Women, Virudhunagar

Love is a magic trap,
No one can escape with a gap.
Love is thorny desire which is pinching like honey drops.
I used to fly like a bird,
But falling like a feather on the ground now.
I was on a dark side
But then realized you as a lamp.
Like peacock feather, fingers will caress you;
Even if it's long distance,
You faded in the brink of my eye but mixed I my soul long back.
I wanna be your vacuum cleaner, breathing in your dust.
Oh! My love
You are my lashes of my eye
You kindled my flame of love.

46
Many Shades Love has
Kaisar Mahmadiftikar Shekh, Anand

Warm and cold, hard and soft
Happy and sad, bold and shy
Oh love ! Oh dear love
Many many shades you have.
In the care of mother, in the scold of father
In the quarrel of brother, in the tease of sister
You are smiling, you are smiling
Oh love! Oh dear love
Many many shades you have.
Sometimes easy, sometimes complicated
Sometimes happy, sometimes sad
You are like weather, changes your shades
You are winter, you are summer
You are monsoon, you are autumn
Oh love! Oh dear love,
Many many shades you have.
Red and black, pink and grey
Words and silence, crowd and emptiness
Oh love! Oh dear Love
Many many shades you have.
In the flute of Lord Krishna, in the pslam of Mirabai
You are smiling, you are smiling
Oh love ! Oh dear love
Many many shades you have.
You make people laugh, you make them cry
You make them proud, you make them shy
Oh Love! Oh dear Love
Many many shades you have.

47
Shades of Love
Madhavi Menon, Holy Cross Institute of Management &
Technology, Calicut

I hardly speak of you,
I would never admit,
How I feel about you,
A beautiful sensation,
Thrills my senses.
Thought it was the words
I fell in love with;
Not the writer.
The incessant conversation,
The simple things you do,
The compliments you pass,
Find myself in a comfort zone,
And bring a smile,
Another version of me.
Thoughts slip out of my grasp,
All explicit.......
I know you don't reciprocate my feelings,
I open my eyes to find
You were never there at all!

48
Love in Being
Dr M Elangovan, Thiagarajar College, Madurai

The shades of love
are infinite and multitude.
Changing their flexible sizes,
they eternally remain
in the deepest niches
of ever-changing, widening hearts.
They carry crores of images
imprinted on gold-layered
divinity and sanctity.
Vast like the ocean;
Flowing like the river;
Growing like the tree;
they take manifestations
of men and women.
They bend, bind
and fluctuating
to give birth to sacredness.
Pristine pure and crystal clear,
love moves beyond eternity.
The shades of love
live in all forms,
all beings and all becomings.
Existence in love is
love in existence.
The shades of love are
aesthetically beautiful
and lovingly lovable.

49
A Reflection on Love
Jayamurali, Sri Sankara Arts & Science College, Kanchipuram
Tamilnadu

Amiable acquaintance affects not heart,
Intimate pals often ignite or calm fire.
Pick property as soul-one, only to thwart;
Purity in soul as only property to tune your lyre.

Untold love lives forever, proclaimed?
Either sheds tear or sustains fear.
Applause in one hand appeals not the claimed;
Chance is a rare child, feel to rear.

Infatuation often infects not our rising swing,
Yet, sure-affection alienated shatters (in) every sense.
Possessive scull stings the owned thing,
Let strange brain be embraced in its very essence!

Mother proves an ideal, not before her death,
Son sets his own utopia to live ever in Dystopia.
Fulfilled one fails not in duty and faith;
Despaired? fails not in vain pursuit and phobia.

Mercy and grace seldom win the life's race;
Hypocrisy and flattery often sustain sound health.
Smile, salutation, gestures, and cry - made of craze.
Hatred, irritation, pressures and wry - born to win wealth.

Be content to travel with your piety to unseen,
But be not indifferent to the suffering seen.
Love be the hymn everywhere, yet, you are to perform.
Let communion and symbiosis be our norm.

50
The Enchanter
L Suriyakala, Sivagangai

There! Hover the blissful blossoms adorning earth,
painted with myriad hues that brings us mirth;
Enchant the flying fairies with a spell of fragrance,
giving no other chance, just with a glance,
leave them in a trance;
Lying there with a vivid blush,
the fairies stay not in a rush,
never want to be out of this delight drenched daze...

Love! As mystic as the arcane nature,
Leaves me in a blissful torture;
Yes! I am a man of iron I bet,
But what if her bait is a majestic magnet?!
Roaming in the woods of love,
Praying the almighty above
to let me be untangled
from the beguiling shades I am tinted of.

Alas! after all, this insane heart of mine,
still yearning for love and let it shine.
This plain page wants to be painted,
But tell me love! What's your shade?
What are U?
An angel?...A Demon?
A delight?...A Disdain?
You are all and All is you.
A blend of abundant shade;
With you, all my logics fade.
At last, of what my soul is made?
Is all of your shade! My love!

51
Shades of Love
Vishnupriya S, Kasturi College of Education

Everyone says….
Be true in…
Be honest with…
Be confidence in…
Be humble with…
Be real in…
Be patience with…
Be good with…
Be kind for…
Be responsible for…
Then, who follows?
Mayn't be everyone…!

52
Love Perfecteth
Nikunj Thaploo, Sector-15 Rohini, near Manav Chowk, Delhi

In heart of heart, this heart repines
To when come that day
O! beloved thou shall be mine.

Not thou when I have
Look how void of day is filled by
from an orchard near by
eat I peach sour and lime
O! without you sweetest of sweet
turns a sour grape.

Then a heart filled with anxiety,
an ocean of gushing tide
finding suddenly myself
at its very shore
then amidst the gale of
winds decipher I a face of one
in hearts of hearts to whom
it calls it's own.

That pretty dame of my sweet dreams
tell me thou when it shall be
I be yours and mine you shall be.
Now, from an orchard to orchid I move
Pluck I roses with thorns unremoved,
to every petal of which I remove
contemplating upon thou be or not be mine.

I amble, I stumble, I roam, I rove
to then the fragrance of jasmine I bow.
Them I pluck one by one
that a garland so pretty
I'll give you one,
putting forth yellow blazing
marigolds at your lotus feet.

With it sun sets the day
Leaving brimmed my heart with
dreams of another day,
the day when this heart
will call aloud
Oh! Pretty mistress, I wait
the day that thou shall be mine.

Trees of Cherry, Trees of Pine
Oh! Someone hear this heart pines
Intoxicated it sings
madly to rhymes of love and life
Oh! Come my beloved
hear these songs of mine
Come to the clutches of my heart
And yours hand in mine.

Go shall we go to some place where
No one shall find no one there
Where you and me shall
Together fare
to far off lands
where neither you and I shall care.

Oh! Thy queen of my heart's throne,
Come now and descend
For the sake of life of my very own.
Thy locks entangle
eyes fascinate
Oh! Me Oh! Me Oh! Me

Thy rosy lips
Congeal the flow
Of the very blood
for a moment
Where my heart stops to know
the very beat of its beat
as if

Ceases my life
to any flow.

Chokes my heart,
eyes my open
in dark of night
whether in dream or in real
not I know
saw the face of someone
now, be it a fairy
, my dream lady
For such is my state
nothing other suits my taste.

But I wait, I wait, I wait
and wait
to that day
When merry between shall us be made.

53
Empress of Words

Arundhuti Chakraborty, Calcutta University, Kolkata

Words,
The ones, I write
which express me
of which I am a wizard.
My colors, with which I paint a picture, and hence a painter.
Those ones which always crowd up in clusters, eager like a
teenager to come out.
Out.
Out of my mind and through my mouth, following their secret
path to my pages.
It's like I own a connoisseur's coveted collection.
Never at loss but granted with a queen's estate at my every
disposal.
Yet,
Yet, until you crossed my path, like a comet star, an unexpected
guest to the night sky.
And I stood there in awe of the celestial marvel.
And this astrophile fell in love with your sight.
Sight,
Which glorify your presence in my dark sky.
As if, my soul slowly blossomed like a late bloomer, finally
blooming, whose season has long passed with spring bidding
adieu, still autumn greeted her, made her a part of her floral
glory.
Evoking in me a musical composition of emotions. Of which I
knew not.
And those emotions like thousand nameless colours of every
possible shade crossed my mind. As if a divine channel of
creation opened. And this stargazer stood there rendering
audience to this phenomenon.
Embraced by the comfort of finally being able to remember the
tune of a long lost dear song.
Song,
I tried to sing the song my soul was listening for the first time.
But I couldn't remember the words of it.

Empress of words was at a loss before her Emperor.
As though every word eluded her, as if they too were
dumbfounded by the queen's newfound beauty. They went in
every direction creating a mayhem, just like her mind was in a
chaos.
The words forgot how to bind themselves in cohesive thoughts
or sentence.
And Empress of words was at a loss.
With no words by her side to aid her expression or command.
That's when she first learnt the language of feelings.
The silent language of feelings. Carved in beautiful silence, they
speak without speaking a syllable, absent yet present. Their
abstract presence laced with tenderness was strong enough for
the communion of the twin souls.
But do you know what happened to the words?
Where did they all go?
Not a word was heard in their town.
Yet they were all there.
They passed each other and everywhere with a tender nod and
flowed between their king and queen effortlessly. The words
joined them in their silent celebration of life. Enveloped in
eternal symphony of love. The words wrapped themselves up in
their new attire of feelings.
The words never spoke again.
They were carefully at rest.
For what use shall words be,
To two hearts speaking the language of love?

54
A Love Like No Other
Vipitha Devi, Paravur, Kollam, Kerala

Two lover who never met each other
But they loved each other intensively.
Each second they lived in hopes
That they will meet each other.
They never complained about each other
And enjoyed their life in full.
Their love was like cold chocolate that
Melts in the warmth of one palm which
Make it sweeter than before.
All around thought their love as fake
As they don't know the love of soul.
Each day their love became fresh and
No ego can destroy its beauty.
Waiting for them was not a burden
As they always lived in their love.

No gifts,
no flowers,
no cards,
no calls,
no messages,
no chats.
They talked in the twinkling of their hearts.
Love in them was not thorns for their path
and it was a thread that coils them tighter.

Everyone was eager to see their meeting.
When they met the whole world
Stood still filled with silence.
Those who saw their meeting had
No words to explain.
Everyone understood that they also
Had these two lovers with them.
The lovers were Life and Death
And their love is Life.

55
Dark Room
Aswathi AS, Thrissur

In the dark room,
He sits and plays
The world's smallest piano.
His fingers compose,
some ancient music,
His music tempts the little lass
who lives nearby a tall tower.
She walks swiftly,
Towards the dark room.
Nor the church gongs,
Nor the light house fog horns could stop her.
Then finally she reaches the dark room.
Frightened by its ambience,
she walks towards the man,
she stands near him,
As if immersed in his divine music.
She gazes at his eyes,
They were inexpressive.
She whispers in his ears,
They were unresponsive.
Suddenly she smells a smoke,
It emanates from the outside window.
Slowly, very slowly, it enters the dark room.
And burns them alive.
A chorus from outside,
Our master told us
To burn him alive.
He was both blind and deaf.

56
Lady Thou Art Free
Amit Pandey, Sidho Kanho Birsha University, Purulia

Lady thou art free; come and go like a soothing day.
Dost thou feel so uneasy with this mundane day?
Hath thy eternal grandeur ever been matched to this summer's
day?'
Lady thou hath snatched the gaiety of the day.
Thy sigh is the panacea to this wounded night.
Ere Goodbyes, thou doth bring nightmare to these forlorn eyes;
though the untold words are yet to tell through the tongue of me;
though the unseen world is yet to see through the eyes of me.
Dear Lady, hath thee ever tried to feel the heartfelt pangs of
Keats?
Hath thee ever tried to read the torn out heart of Heathcliff?
Oh! Lady, invisible fairy demon are thee.
The sky is in its merry, floral fragrance does it carry.
But, alas! thy tantalizing hair makes it ugly.
Lady thou art free.

57
Ocean of Love
Kavya S Mony, Thiruvananthapuram

Thud..!
A thunderous plunge resonated
in the cold deserted beach.
Red colour crept the creamy sand.
Bruised was him, bleeding.
Wan moonlight was his sole company.
Thousands of miles away,
I heard his helpless moan.
A frail cry from a loved one
wakes you up with frightening thud.
Be it a tormenting thought
or a discomforting dream,
solace has to be found within.
The smile of aurora whispered to me:
'Whatever evil has to happen to him,
let it all occur in your dreams
and spare him.'
And this ray of hope is called Love.
If Potter was saved from all evil
by Lily's Love,
Won't he too be secure,
in the deep ocean of my love?

The ocean of love

Magical, it is, the shore of Love.
Once we enjoy the beauty of it,
nothing can pull us back.
The waves in the ocean cleanses
the dirt ridden in our hearts.
Be it ego, disrespect, anger.
The serene touch of love purifies us,
just like the tiny white bubbles
washes the seashore with vigour.
Myself elevated with his bottomless love,

and himself sanctifying from mine.

Diving more and more into its depths,
do we find hidden treasure.
Is it the Peridot stones of Hawaiian lands?
Or the Aquamarian gems?
Gems are unique, so are we.
Love shows us who we are,
a process of understanding sets in.

In the middle of the ocean,
he asked me once,
'How do you understand peace?'
Stood I, clueless, gaping at his eyes,
which signaled an appalling danger.
'You appreciate peace more in violence.'
The raging sea and her elements of anger –
the thunderous storm and lightning,
cannot be quietened that easily.
The best way to protect ourselves
is to board the boat of Trust.
As long as the boat doesn't wretch,
so are we.
The winds ate the sails, roars
and everything it would find.
But an unknown force protected
us, nay.. our boat.
We called it- Unconditional love.

The day after the storm, we smiled happily
sharing small pieces of joy
fished from the ocean.
Irony, it is, when love is imagined
as complex phenomenon,
its very essence lies in its
simplicity of sharing the mirth.

58
Let Not Let Me Die
Debarpita Roy, Birati, Nazrul Path, Kolkata

Embargo your leisure on my lips; tired of making
love with your name,
Gone is my passion on your charm, nor to retreat
from your flickering flame.
Enchanted was I; rather bewitched by your
voluntary manly game,
Though you're right, women have always cited
excuses lame.

Oh! your words perforated into my sprouted breast
I kept quiet, you could flee lest.
Neither you nor could I put love to test;
You never know I placed you innocuously at the crest.

It was not you who raffled me like a possession,
But the monstrous plague of your share of obsession.
Eventually you might have changed to be someone's
best decision,
Though I assure you she should have sought
a long-term precaution.

The day you look back into the departed me,
Left will be nothing but a handful of plea.
And I shall be found to be ostentatiously free,
Unfortunately you'll be checkmated to the lives of three.

59
~Toxic Relationships~
Noor Fathima VN, MGAJ Arts and Science College N Paravur
Ernakulam

Alas!
Love has this drastic phase
Which is a maze
Of illusions
Where we can't find ourselves
And something going to
Haunt you till the end
Ouch!
It is so painful
And so full of side effects
Chaotic and brain eating
And something that
Tangled up your life lines
Hey!
It will drown you
To the depth of this
Uncomfortable sensations and nightmares
And something which give you
An ache which can't cure
Indeed!
It is a labyrinth of lies
That make things toxic and traumatic
It is more like rhetorical questions and melancholy
And something
Hopeless and exhaustingly exhausting.

60
A Love So Intact

Udatha Geetanjali, MMK & SDM College for Women, Mysuru
Karnataka

As we pass through the streets
"What is trust?" She asks.
I sing "That lovely smile a child has when a parent tosses them
in the air".
"What is respect?" She asks.
I sing "That great pleasure in saluting those ambitious souls
fighting at the border".
"What is passion?" She asks.
I sing "That zeal shining in the eyes of an athlete to excel in the
sport".
"What is kindness?" She asks.
I sing "That person who owns nothing more but still tries to pour
his all into others".
"What is caring?" She asks.
I sing "That one good mate who walks hand in hand through
every hurdle".
"Then what is love?" She asked.
I sing "Aren't trust, respect, passion, kindness, caring different
shades of love".
With a delightful look on the face we sing together "Yes, they
are indeed. When people out there are occupied in replacing
shades of sunglasses and lipstick let us try to sow the seed of
love eternally".
Rest assured.

61
Falling in Love

Chetna Bhagoji, SKE'S Govindram Seksaria Science Degree
College, Belagavi

What about me,
What about you,
When you fall into love, this is what happens!
Her talks
Her laughter
Even-though she is not near, she is near.
Playing with her life
she is simply displeased.
Suddenly seeing her in dreams,
Having bath in the naughty rain,
What about me, what about you,
When you fall into love, this is what happens!
Slowly she pushed her hair behind
Was that her left hand or the right?
We remember everything like the packed clouds,
She is there in the heart but try to forget her;
WHAT ABOUT ME, WHAT ABOUT YOU, WHEN YOU
FALL INTO LOVE, THIS IS WHAT HAPPENS!!!!!

62
You're the One
Mohana A, K S Rangasamy College of Arts and Science,
Tiruchengode

My eyes are looking for you
like next to me,
I count the days
between you and me.

I know,
I'm brave,
When I see you
I'm like a spider silk.

Even we're miles apart
I can feel your touch,
Like holding entire universe,
When I felt alone our memories helped me to set my soul free.

I don't want to roll away from you,
because you're the
beamed of my jewel,
colors of my rainbow.

63
Wondrous Love
RT Renikha Lettish, Holy Cross College, Nagercoil

Love is the evidence of divine existence,
That cannot be tarnished, white-washed
Or replaced. In fall, storm or
Winter does she stand;
The filth and wounds she neither complain
Nor, do we see her cry?
She puts her fence around the globe;
Promising to care, soothe and abide.
Even to the unreachable part she exists!
And the valley of silence
Is full of her wonders.
She is not greedy nor keeps predictions;
And her shade will leave us in awe!
Her existence is her choice.
Through thick and thin she stands,
Though, we are unworthy of her-
Yet; her root deep and secure,
She burn for legacy!
So bright, so dazzling,
Her timid friends come together;
From nooks and corners,
To see her burn with love!
Oh! Such wonderful thing called 'love'
Exist; the beauty of undying love;
Though we see her a thousand times,
She never ever grow old,
The world is filled with her shade,
With every sight we see her live!
Oh! What a wonderful, wonderful.

64
Shades of Love
Neena Paul, Anakkara

The mind is freely floating
with the mind, the trees are shedding last orange leaves.
Suddenly, the spring arrives with love
mind enchant with love.

But then, I wandered into light and to darkness,
in search of my love.
Still am in dilemma, I found different shades of
love throughout the journey.
Some shades are strange, few are like fiction,
yet some delight like spring, it made blossom.
But when the summer arrives, only memories left.
As Santiago; finally I found the real treasure of love.
"its with me"

65
Krishna, My Love
M Soni, Gudimalkapur, Hyderabad

There comes, our little love,
The darling of Brindavan,
Playing with cattle and dove,
Dancing with cowherds along,
Laddus, butter, rice, appams,
Feeding each other generously,
Naughty smiles and mischievous games,
With the Lord to take care earnestly

Don't' tell Yasodha, O Ramaa!
For she don't know who Kanha is,
It's only a matter of love Dharti maa,
That he is creating a Leela by eating bits,
Stopped by strong hold of mom,
The little Krishna smiled,
Showed the entire Universe without a mum,
In little mouth with Yasodha shocked

Dark blue Yamuna flows aside,
To the wonderful flute tunes,
The covey Radha sits like a bride,
The lovely damsels moving on the dunes,
Scintillating moonlight flows on,
Par with the blue and white streams,
The whole universe get drunk on,
Spread the world with wonderful dream

Black, orange, purple and red,
Caught by mindful illusions,
Lay there the Kaliya's head,
With lost energy and visions,
With wives in tens surrounded,
Stood humbly and low,
As the Lord's feet got stamped,
On its' hoods and glided slow

One Hundred Shades of Love

The panic-struck Kamsa sat,
Aside on his golden throne,
Alas! The mighty elephant lies flat,
And the muscular wrestlers groan,
The savage king quivers,
Mukunda made a move robust,
Filled the room with shivers,
The cruel monarch tastes the dust

Arise! Awake! Arjuna!! Show your valour,
Do not get cast down,
With illusions and worldly allure,
You are the chosen one!!
Trust no one, except Me,
Pick up the arrow and bow,
I can clear all your plea,
Spring up the law bough

Eighteen days to go!
The war of blood and flesh hiss,
In the conches that blow,
There is no chance to miss,
Revolt, repression and disgust,
So many emotions hurt,
Ruled by unjust and distrust,
Painted the Kurukshetra art

Holding the harmony ties close,
In heart, soul and mind,
With his satchel and emotional overdose,
Sudama's tears made him blind,
Krishna graced with friendly hug,
Washed his feet, served food,
Covered him with a golden rug,
Remembered all moments of good

Awesome, comforting, benevolent,
Unconditional is God's love,

For the mankind that is indolent,
A boon coming from skies above
A solace for the restless souls,
Who belong to the disturbing land,
Look upon the Krishna as a whole,
To guide you with a magical hand

66
Praising and Probing
Sagar B, DOSR in English, Tumkur University, Tumkur
Karnataka

A queen of Ice Fort
You are deserved for mere Court

When you were Born
The world took a Turn

Until now life is thorny Dumb
From now it turns to Stardom

Lamentation is at zenith for Disappearance
When do I expect your unhoped Reappearance

Seldomly, I see You
Frequently, I miss You

I've been searching you around Hill
Probing and posing across Honey Hill

The finding day will be pleasant one
Aftermath we will be concerted one

67
Shades of Love
Nzimiro Lazarus Ugo, University of Nigeria, Nsukka, Enugu
Nigeria

Barely visible, as the Blue Ridge Mountains unveiled without a
noise
were tiny beautiful riffs born in antiquity
blind but guides, dumb, with it's tone deeper than the hues of
red, black and white's voice.
gliding on the winds of sacrifice to disperse blessed serenity.

There I lay, dying of heat and thirst even near the Nile,
by the dunes, atop my own pyramids of bile;
from Angel Falls descended it's elixir without guile
and effortlessly razed eons of venomous pile.

When wrecked by the aisled reefs beneath the mammoth Uluru
and death loomed from the cold winds of the dead ends -not
Uguru,
it's shades they were that kept me warm
and it's droplets of affectionate-compassion, the cloak I had
worn.

Then came the great wars of mighty towers
to the horrors from snowcapped peaks for unending hours,
again it gilds like a shadow with the force of mighty running
waters on speedy-wings across the seven borders
restoring lost sparkles which it utters.

Battered I lay me down to weep,
My place, peace and soul shattered by much rift;
alone, I launched for the deep
and would have been gone, sunken, but for a little love's timely
lift.

My pride, hate and fear,
these wounds, all man's manacles which I bear
as through treacherous uncertainties of life's current I fare;

love again my drabby-scrawny-lot-with-dreary-eyes beheld to
bring intervention,
it's gracious beauty patching me up in its shady attention.

Though this game I start afresh,
by little love's tender touch I stand refreshed
and my eyes opened-not to life's illusory notions of race, praise
and power,
but to see disjointed hopes and cheers soldered by the hour.

It's tiny spark is all we need for our fire,
of these lies and borders let's make a pyre
and by her wings perch atop pinnacles of real freedom if we
heed,
to behold the truth rise from the embers
overlooking the innermost ties of all members,
that; 'we all have it in us, Shades of Love, all we need'.

68
The Flightless Pin
Rounak Barman, The University Of Calcutta

So close, yet again?
Stay silly balloon stay.
Hurt you'll if you stray carelessly close.
Don't you see?
Tales aren't made for strays like us.
Few have written tales for the kind of us.
Balloons and pins only fall if they kiss,
Only fall when they know yet they risk.

You love them best when you let them fly,
Watch them clothe the sky!
At least one has to keep their head and hold
Itself down and yet make room for the other
To play in the barren ground.

I will laugh with you just the same
Even when it hurts inside.
I'll laugh silly balloon from a cold distance
Yet you'll fly knowing I never loved you.
You'll fly, someday realising
Love tales aren't quite just.

Buried deep in the ground,
I'll keep admiring you and think of how
Tales aren't made for the like of us.

Yet someday when you descend again,
I'll laugh with you just the same.
When you ask, "What have you been up to?"
I'll say-
"I kept searching for a lonely pin lost like I."

69
Shades of Love
Trayambika RN, MMK & SDM College for Women, Mysuru

My heart skipped a beat
When my eyes met yours
Little did I know
I'm falling in love
Honey brown wild
Sparkling eyes
Oh dear!
What a beauty you are
All the time, all the day!
Maybe I would be in love with you forever
Little did I know I hate myself ever
Everything I had been through
Everything I had suffered
I hid it with my smile
No one would know
No one could wonder
My anxiety creeped in
I was losing my breath
Consumed by fear
I went restless
My heartbeat accelerated
And I was numb
Flashbacks of me suffering
Getting bullied
Crying in silence
Afraid to be alone
Thoughts of self harm
Crawled into me
Little did I know
I would get though this
Little did I know
If it happened, it was needed
Little did I know
I wanted to accept and heal
And there you were to realise me that

Love is being kind to oneself first
It all begins with oneself
If you haven't loved yourself completely
You can't love another person
Perceiving the truth with you
Every day is an adventure!
Every day is a blessing.

70
Shades of Love
S Arnisha Thangam, Holy Cross Home Science College
Thoothukudi

You picked me when I had nowhere to go
You left me when I had somewhere to go
My feelings for you is so many to let go
Just as hard as to unpuzzle my lego
I was empty without a scent
I would rather not blame or lament
My love for you goes round and round why do I keep coming
back
Should I call some referee to keep my track
On the melody where even your warmth has now been reserved
The film I had with you was preserved
You became the person I loved too much
You became the person I was entwined too much
The shades of our love is deeper than any rift
Just give me my last gift
So that I can't go back anymore
Free me from this abyss Mon Amore.

71
Shades of Silence
M Saye Soozie, Annanagar, Chennai

Forever is the sea, though each wave dies
Eternal is Time, even as moments fleet by
Tall stands the mountain, even as each tree falls
You live on my dearest in the memories of my heart.

Youth flowed like grains of sand, together yet distinct
Years rolled by as witness, when our life soared or kinked
Like the droplets of water, strong was our bond
That we blended together and braved all storms.

Moments of shared sunsets in the comfort of Silence
Playful waves at our feet; Nature, love's license
Paved the way to that niche, where our hearts beat as one
It was a long journey, to reach this Golden Sun.

Was it God's fury? Did the cosmos connive?
To wrench from us our soul? But had us beguiled?
Muted voice, Lifeless limbs, ebbing life, dwindling breadth
My love lay well-nigh lifeless, with borrowed time from Death

Mother's role I donned, second time in life
To care for a grown-up infant, who'd lost the power to cry
I held him in my prayers, I held him in my heart
Holding back my tears, I embraced him with my thoughts
The Strong became the weak; the weak strong
An eerie silence remained, after he'd long gone

Life ends in death, but Love goes on
And I play the legions of love
Drawing from my treasured memories
Silence, there is, but now not so eerie
Love taught me Silence and its Vagaries

72
Sensual Raisins
Hridyesha Gogoi, Cotton University

Her earlobes are ripe with berries
Dangling from a string, thin like
The papery dreams of her siesta.
Winter must be here!
Her lips are blue and dry,
Our plates are crowded with
Sliced fruits except for the
Juicy ones for we might devour
Like savages and to stain our starched
Shirts is what we cannot afford
In this afternoon of pallid despair.

With her woodpecker like precision
She carved me out, an intricate design
Of love in its highest crescendo.
She's like a walking tavern
Reeking of needy visitors and cheap liquor
With a heart of an avocado
And eyes like an archaic language
Lost in transmission.
Yet she has a way of absorbing souls
As she lets her mouth wide open
Reducing the spectator into
A transparent object of lunacy.

It's that day of the month again
With a wicker basket and a bandana
To keep her wicked bangs from
Swaying in the tropical air,
She moves towards the gateway
The red lipstick has started to melt
In the blazing sun
Dripping all over her blouse
With peach prints.
It is not winter yet.

73
Love has many Shades that never Fade
Dhara Teraiya, Porbandar

Love is worship!
Love shapes in worship,
When two persons are in love,
They always remember each other in their prayer.
Love has many shades that never fade!
Love is blind!
Love is blind because,
Mother loves her child before
She can hold and embrace that tiny one.
Love has many shades that never fade!
Love is oneness!
It is connection of pure
Soul and Heart, that never part.
Love has many shades that never fade!
Love is infatuation!
Love is infatuation of staying together till the
Last breathe of each other, a thought of never see sad to each
other.
Love has many shades that never fade!
Love is attraction!
Attraction of thoughts that wants
To feel pure and Unconditional sacrifices.
Love has many shades that never fade!
Love is hope!
Yes, finding a beautiful tree in the
Middle of desert, Love require that much hope.
Love has many shades that never fade!

74
Love Par Excellence

Meenashy V, Shree Raghavendra Arts and Science College
Chidambaram

The first ever shade for everyone
Commences from their mother's womb
Such a protective and peaceful slumber that one
Can enjoy in the midst of gloomy womb
Shade of love from mother is a durable one!

Love is like a Banyan Tree's shade
At times every aerial prop roots begins to fade
None can swing to one, Time and Experience will make
To realize, which root holds us more in all our aches
Shade of love from mother is a durable one!

Too much of anything is good for nothing
Love Too, if more injected creates ecstasy
But suddenly, if less injected destroys everything
Beware! Love is Destroyer and Preserver of humanity
Shade of love from mother is a durable one!

From the womb, to the Tomb
One shade will always protect us
It is Selfless, Soulful and Sacred shade
That will never ever fade forever
Shade of love from mother is a durable one!

75
Palette of Love
Sonali Sharma, Raipur Road, Dehradun, Uttarakhand

In every piece of a memorable idea
That holds me an inch closer
To all the different wonderful spots
In my journey of life
I figure your name
On the candles floating nearer
As supreme candlelight.
In the ardent mornings
When the light heat
Smoothens the folds of tablecloth
I bury the whiteness of it
Under a double fringed artwork
The black outlines on which
Captivate my faint desire
And quotes the longingness
Of my shaded life.
In the mysterious dark nights
When the glistening moonlight
Makes love to the cold breeze
I look into the engraved letters
The red ink on which
Bursts into my veins as faithful love
Emerges as a soft blush on skin
I will joyfully intermingle with
Different shades
On the palette of love.

76
A Butterfly's Flutter
Dr Aparna Ajith, Assistant Professor in English at SNCW
Kollam

I felt a new life sprouting within me,
Filling my fading dawns like a honeybee.
I can quiet surmise
A nascent surprise.
Your twitching keeps me alive,
Yearning for my little love to arrive.
I feel your muted love in the flapping,
Craving for your entry in a snowy wrapping.
I linger in your butterfly tickles,
Your zigzags stir my trickles.
When I feel a '*gulu gulu*' in my belly,
It's my '*golu molu*' moving around like a jelly.
You nestle in my heart's rhythm,
My epiphany for you has no algorithm.
My winter craves for your love's spring,
My endless heart rhymes are set to sing.
My feelings ratify their connections with you,
Annexing my sweet and sour cadences within you.
Counting down days for my fluttering butterfly
To stretch the tender wings and soar high!

77
Shades of Love

Srijana Subedi, Tribhuvan University
Central Department of Statistics, Kirtipur, Nepal

For the pure soul, whom you can trust undoubtedly;
For those sincere eyes, where you can visualize emotions
proudly;
For those hearts, which never departs despite hindrance;
For that togetherness, filled with love, care, & patience;
The shade of love, which we always should be grateful for!

For that love, which is elevated like the height of Himalaya;
For that love, which is as deep as the Mariana Trench;
For that love, which is as fine as twenty-four-carat gold;
That love, which is as pure as the newly born baby's soul;
The shade of love, which we always should be grateful for!

For that love, which gives strength and encouragement;
For that bond, which encompasses excessive merriment;
Love is so sweet, the beautiful song of a heartbeat;
For that love, which can understand the pain behind difficulties;
The shade of love, which we always should be grateful for!

78
Shades of Hope in Pandemic Regime
Ranjitha Roy, Warsaw, Poland

(Her version...)

Ignored initially, then an Epidemic
Feared dreadfully, now a Pandemic

Stretched with pace at its best
in the East and the West

Do you see what is brought
Not a true dearth nor a drought

but cognizance of worth and wealth
of one's *life, love and health*

When the utterly swift world
with all the thoughts whirled

Chose to take a pause
understandably, for a cause

Leverage the time to gather
mandated distance in between, yet together

To share the pun and the pain
to not lose hope to fly again

Difficult to comprehend
Not permitted to pretend

Admit I'm scary
Not a desired fairy

With the *deadline* of this episode unknown
many shades of life *reportedly* shown

Strategic seems no move
tactical is no groove

Let me go away, let me go away
with freedom laid out all the way

Bid me a bye, bid me a bye
Realize *life is definitely worth a try*

79

Love's Shades Shed: True Shade Never to Fade
Reminiscences of Experiences
Dr DR Pratima Roy, St Joseph's Junior Degree and PG College
for Women, Kurnool

Parents trove on me, cuddling
Siblings crave for me, hugging
Friends rave in flurry, feasting
All's love sparry: 'Tis spotting
Pure, fun, *sans* blurry, toying
But in love truly showing
Till childhood parry…passing

Then came fragrance fancied youth
All masked in sweet perfumed breath
The love between you and me
Made a wonderful alchemy
You gate-crashed into my life
I struggled what to name it
Only to know it's craze

Silently, but grown in thought-
Joined my soul-mate for life
Travelled both in sun and rain
Left he me in dusk of life
To Hea'nly realm, ne'er to come
Burying his love for me
Breaking my heart in lament

I've learnt the lessons of love,
Passed by diverse shades of love
Filial love, fleeting love,
Conjugal love, children's love
Little thought I that God's love…
That AGAPË was true love
It made me pass thro' life's strife!

80
Shades of Love
Pooja K Odedra, Rajivnagar, Porbandar

Actually! What is love?
Love is a feeling, a thing of
Beauty is a joy forever
Your love makes my life
Colourful. I feel like colour of
Love were blasting on me
In pain also I never feel sad
I always feel happy
And I forget all my pain
When I see my love, my soul mate
With me. When I close my eyes
L feel you, I can see you, feel you
From bottom of my heart, my sole
My body is not working
Because of my heart
But my body is working
Because in my heart you have
A precious place there
You are the person who give me
Name, image and a personality
My whole world is around you
You are the only person who makes
My world complete
And nobody can love you like me
A shade of our love spreads
Far high in the sky and
Far away from world
Just to say I love you
Never seems enough
But to express how much I
Love you is the thing which
Matter for love. The different-different
Shades of my love always spreads on
you. " I LOVE YOU A LOT MY LOVE "!
I love you now more than ever before.

81
Hues of Hope
Sharanya H, Adi Sankara Training College, Kalady

Into the darkest caverns she slumped,
Decked in dejection
Confined to the dark mocking faces of melancholy;
She calibrated with the rhythm of agony.

Writhed in woe,
Permeated in panic,
With an unquenchable thirst for acceptance;
She anticipates for a soothing breeze to fondle her soul.

An ecstatic lustre encapsulated her yearning eyes
That danced at the glimpse of the unexpected.
Her lips parched to speak,
Her hopes heaved once again.

Her obscured persona glistened again,
Through her veins gushed incessant happiness
Dribbles of joyful tears oozed out;
And he kissed it to perish.

Elixir of love cascaded like a flowing river
That ardently caressed the excruciating agonies
Embracing her vigorous hopes,
She smiled at last.

The quilt of pains and miseries unveiled,
Clogged pores widened into new horizons
Embellished in ecstasy,
She strides sanguinely to taste the nectar of life.

Debris of the raped body buried,
She drenched in the magic spell of his love
And surged like a phoenix bird,
Yearning to reside in the infinite shade of love.

82
Break-Off
Rasmi Menon, Ummanazhi, Palakkad, Kerala

I think, I know not the ways into the wilderness,
but when I was forsaken in the garden of remembrance
I wished, what if my ears were buried in my heart beats
and I knew the less-trodden ways back Home...

One day, out of the blue,
when I was out of the world, fit as a fiddle in fact,
they blasted that I "didn't make it";
and the waves of my heart took an ever-sleeping line.

Some mysteries live in the catacomb,
only known to those under cover...
a love of eternal flair,
between the soul and the corse.

Perching on the headstone,
awaiting those fallen, ahead of time
I dreamt of redemption, for that budding bag of bones
reposing in the crypt...

I had been seeking relentless love,
through all my flying years...
I seize it now—behind time
pointlessly here in this God's acre—
the love I have for the throb of the heart,
for the blink-of-an- eye and for the queer gush of blood...

and I think, what if I break off my trip to that wilderness!!!

83
Vermilion
Smita Kishore, NSCB PG College Lucknow

I accepted you with this vermilion,
The day we got tied in this holy union,

You took a stake in my sorrow and joys,
While I looked at you with demure eyes,

The holy, heavenly and pious mingle,
Made our whole lives shuffle,

Those inane and naïve fights,
Those tiring and restless nights....

Taught and gave lessons of a lifetime,
Pain made this ordeal sublime,

With anguish and vengeance end,
Life continued but didn't contend....

Pretense ended with the hopeful love
A new enticing belief was just enough,

Lessons learnt and understood,
Taught how to overlook,

With scars on the soul, we fly ahead,
Leaving behind the acrimony dread,

The soulmates blend and come back to each other,
Disowning the hollow life forever....

84
Finite Flesh and Love
Bibu Binu Thomas, Pondicherry University, Puducherry

From blue to black
The change in colour was well visible
In his face and in the face of the sky.

Smile and bright teeth of a pale woman
Played in the background with audio,

The video is old, the television is old and old is that woman
Old is that man whose face colour has changed,
He is the one who is penning this
While wiping oozing phlegm.

The television is working in the absence of sensations
Something which he has lost long ago,
Along with that missing woman
About whom he talks, watch and talks more.
Alone, his blabberings ended.

There are no hormones left in him
Actions are dead and so is dopamine.
He is reluctant to be the pursuer of happiness.

Today is the tenth anniversary of her death
He celebrated it by masturbating on their videos of joy.
Pleasure was absent, it was dull and void
Hollowness, in his mind and in his flesh.
The video is happy,
she is filled with grace and life.
He has rotten,
It is nothingness and death and still, he breathes.

85
Care is Love: Shade of Love
Kapil Semwal, IGNOU, Uttarkashi

On a rainy rainy day, mother holds an umbrella
over a child, wetting herself in the rain,
it's care, shade of love.
On a result day, dad scolds a child who scored less marks,
it's worry about future, shade of love.
On a mischievous day, sister scoldes a younger brother, not to
fast drive a bicycle,
It's care, shade of love.
On a cold cold evening, lover wear his coat to his girlfriend,
It's care, shade of love.
On a friendship day, friend tie a friendship belt on the hand of
his friend,
It's friendship, shade of love.
On an anniversary day, children surprise their parents with a
cake,
It's love, shade of love.
From Sweet to Salty, Pungent to Spicy,
From Bitter to Sweet, Sweet to Bitter
All are care, shades of love.

86
The Drizzle of Love
Krishangi Sarma, B Borooah College, Dr Bhubaneswar
Guwahati, Assam

In the deepest corners
of my heart,
a colour, oh so rich
penetrates through the layers
and paints a visage on my bare chest.
I hold no guilt and no shame
as I let every shade,
run deep through the crevices of my body.

Seasons pass by,
and in the nakedness of my soul,
a garden takes birth.
Amidst the pansies and poppies;
chrysanthemums and lavenders,
A hundred poetry come alive,
all of them, smeared
with the shades of love.

Time flows, perennially;
Dawn to dusk,
Dusk to dawn,
whilst, in embraces I find a sea of hues.
Some celebrate the vibrancy of life,
while some, mourn the dullness.
Unabashed they carry on with their stories,
filling the canvas,
manifesting a deal, so great,
for what are we all without love,
and what is love without us all.

87
Shades of Love
Anagha V, Mysuru Makala Kota & Shri Dharmasthala Girls
College, Mysuru

You were a new hope that rose in my life,
You were the star in the darkest nights,
You were in my dreams holding my hand and standing by my
side,
I hoped this dream would never end.

You came in my life as a rain in a desert,
But I should've known that clouds flew away with breeze;
I thought you were laughing at my jokes,
Now I know that it was over my stupidity.

I was feeling as if I was on the top of the world with you,
And now you have left me in the world with only darkness.
I was clearly picturing my future with you,
Now you have made me someone who can't even picture her
present.

No matter whose mistake it was, I would always apologize,
So that our relation wouldn't end;
I should have understood that your love was a game,
When you didn't even try;

I just hope you got someone who loves you like me,
Every time I think, you may want me to come back,
But I am afraid that I will be wrong.
I wish that she doesn't play games like you did to me.

I won't let you succeed in your intentions,
Now I had made my heart of stone and my mind is focused on
my career;
I know I am broken but now I can't feel any pain,
I am happy for what you did to me,
Because now I know I won't fall for it again.

88
My Beginning, End and Ever-After
Suji S, National Engineering College, KR Nagar, Kovilpatti

A heart of wish was a piece of sandwich.
Once I requested a sandwich,
I was denied and thrown away.
I set my heart on it.
But they refused me to eat.
I screamed, cried, dejected myself.

They caged me inside the walls.
I lost happiness.
A light of you emerged into my life.
You smiled at me.
I was frustrated and depressed.
The way I went was rigorous.

The only thing which made me move
That's You.
In every situation, you gave me hands.
You filled every relationship in my life.
Whenever I feel alone, you were my aid.
You returned the perforated happiness.

You were my consolation.
You made me realize that,
The time spent in the cage was
To attain the most precious one day.
I was mad that love depends on money.
Love is all about Lust.

So, I refused it from my life.
But I dreamt.
But you visualized that love lies in words.
And you said, "I'm always there for you."

You are the feature of my future,
I longed for you.

You turned me a creature,
I experienced an adventure.

You re-emerged the thoughts of love,
I fell in love with you.
You are ethereal of all,
I'm pleased to have you.

89
Shades of Love
Reena Joseph, St Ann's Degree College for Women, Mallapur

I can see her smile, her beauty as I gaze,
To her beautiful eyes and her angelic face,
My heart was wishing to meet her eyes and hold a stare,
But there she goes looking at someone else
just like having an affair.
I tried to come near her then I smile,
As I come forward I can see her as a woman who waits as I walk
down in the isle,
I can clearly see my future with her as a loyal and true lover,
But her eyes spoke and said we're not meant for each other.
It was an unrequited love, with different shades I must state,
Because of her who held my heart's key can only give a sojourn,
I could never make my precious someone to stay,
So I shall let my only happiness go and walk away.
Now my love is happy with another man,
A man who owned her heart right from the start,
I watched them smile and held each other's hand,
Exchanging vows " I love you till ' death do us apart."

90
Bitterness of Love
Mary Jeniffer Samuel, Pondicherry University, Puducherry

My voice screamed in a lonely place,
Searching for a genuine love;
Why is love so bitter?
My strange mind enquired,
Like lightning in the sky;
My thoughts flashed,
Bringing down a thunderous rain
To unveil the truth,
The story of a lost love
Filled with grief in my heart,
In open-air,
A mixture of complete hatred puffed with smoke,
Growing in bitterness with a smile,
A mask of fake love,
By leaving the ripples of anguish and insecurity,
A mortal relationship,
An ultimate result of sober and pain
Not again of simple love,
But just kisses, flamed with the bitterness of love,
Satisfaction of needs
By injecting the venom of betrayal in love.

91
Being and Becoming
Shwetha RS, Lady Doak College, Tallakulam, Madurai

She blushed gently
As she opened her eyes
He stood before her
With a bright red rose
Their eyes met
Hearts possessed
Love they say it is.
Of which I know not sure

Love it is for sure
When She holds you in her arms
Close to her chest
As she feeds you with her breast
To silence your shrill cries

Love it is for sure
When She smiles as you kick
With tiny and soft toes
Tears well up in her eyes
Watching you grow big

Love it is for sure
When He carries you on his shoulders
As well as in his heart
He guides you through the dark
Moulding you to become bolder.

Love it is for sure
When He pains himself with glee
Just to keep you smiling
He walks with you and guides you
By His words and deeds

Love it is for sure
Love in its purest form.

92
When it's Love
Sakshi Dubey, Amity University, Noida

for when he held her compassionately...
she knew it was love
for how he held her when she was wrecked to the core,
inconsolable...
she knew it was love
for when he fell deep into her eyes...
she knew it was love
for when he dreamed of her, embraced her in those soulful
nights...
she knew it was love
for how he unfolded himself in front of her...
she knew it was love
for all those nights she went breathless...
she knew it was love
for when she sat galvanized in front of him...
she knew it was love
for when she longed that insatiable desire to be with him...
she knew it was love
for when she lost herself in the reveries of their past...
she knew it was love
its when their memories, past reminisences kept her alive...
she knew it was love
for she was not afraid of falling for the very first time
however, she didn't wanted to fall if it was so soon...

93
Gods That Surround You
Sonal Maharana, NES Ratnam College, Bhandup (W), Mumbai

You say, "There is no God",
"Open your eyes and look around you,"
The men in white, the men in brown and the men in blue,
These are the Gods that surround you.

Things are tough, I can understand,
It can never be easy; fighting a pandemic,
But these people, they prove us wrong,
The men in uniform, "The alchemic",
That's what they are called,
They tell us to stay strong.

Saving thousands of lives, as they put their own at risk,
They can't even meet their family or hug their kids,
And when you ask, "What's keeping you away from them?"
They smile serenely and reply, "My patients, who are still sick."

You throw stones at them, call them names,
Beat them, and say words you never should,
Taking all the abuse, they wear their PPE kit like a cape,
Instead of outrage, they smile and nod and never blame.

You say, "I can't breathe in this mask,"
Their problems you never understand,
"Stay home, stay safe," it is all they ever ask.
The man that sanitized the malls, cinema and the roadside,
He didn't have enough money to feed his kids,
And yet when you ask, "Why are you risking your life?"
"It is my duty to my nation," he says with pride.

If you tell me that there are no Gods,
I would again repeat the same words,
Look around you,
There are Gods that surround you.

94
Wish List
Shehnaz Gujral, Salmiya, Kuwait

I wish a luxurious life, Simple living with no strife.
Brands and boutiques ain't the posh.
Slave free of inane fame.

I wish to be with me this lockdown.
Locking the cyber space for a serene space.
No net will mollycoddle me the best.

I wish to break chasm of virtual and real.
No what's app from the alienated world of work.
Fluttering my new wings of joy.

I wish to bury the keys kissing the browser.
Group tasks are like a chain gang.
Updating soft wares in wary windows.

I wish no checks from the circle of cheques.
Tears and laughter, I serve in blogs.
Web page is the cobweb of mind clogs.

I wish a dial telephone and a time piece to set.
Watching sunrise and sunset holding cozy hands.
Chasing butterflies and paradise in land of sands and castles.

95
** Love's Funeral **
Ramsha Zaheen, IGNOU, New Delhi

Oh Please! Don't disturb me now
I'm at a funeral
Cremating my feelings for you
Burying them deep inside my heart
At the same place
Where once we exchanged
Our vows
In the same black dress
With same black shade of love
Which you gifted me

A coffin is here
Of your favourite chocolate Box
And in that, with the corpse of feelings, lie
Some dried rose petals of our first valentine's day
Your broken love band,
Some scattered beads of my necklace
A white shirt with your cologne
Your cracked spects
The strap of your watch
Our old photographs
Few love letters,
Some stolen kisses
Numerous warm hugs
Some unvoiced truths

I'm not alone here
Your treachery
Your violence
Your lies
Your dominance
Are here to Console me
They are wiping out my tears
And saying that
Tomorrow I will definitely be happy

After seeing those scars
Which you have given me
On my heart
Because scars have made me strong
And told me that you were wrong
If I could bother that cruelty and pain
Surely I'm not gonna face that again
A Satanic insane.

96
Your Love for Me
Punita, Rajpura, Jind, Haryana

Your love for me is like
Melting ice on the Himalayas
Flowing like rivers
From you to me
Wide, deep and calm
It increases the ocean of my heart
And makes my heart
Wider, deeper and calmer
Your love is like heavy rains
In the plains of India
It starts slowly
Drop by drop
The showers come like delicious waves
Becoming sweeter and sweeter
Wet me like some heavenly liquor
Pouring down upon me
My soul becomes
Itself a slight drop of rain
And melts within the very sum of you
Becomes an inseparable part of you
Your love is like the desert of Thar
Very wide and vast
Only sand flows here and there
It becomes hotter at noons
And burns very inside of me
But at nights
Becomes cooler and cooler
And sooths my soul
To very deep inside it
It becomes like
Living in solitude for you
And you become
The whole universe for me.

97
In Love with Own Self!

Shweta Ghanshyam Punjabi, JG College of Commerce
Ahmedabad

And one day looking at the sky,
Finding myself too high to fly.
I came across a droplet of water,
That makes me feel not to be shy.
When a couple loves each other,
in the way they stay,
I love myself, in the way I slay.
Searching for self in the rest of the world,
I found myself in the best of the word.
Loving someone to make them glad,
Love your own to make yourself clad.
Leaves of the tree that fall in the autumn,
Fall for yourself in all the seasons to blossom.
Be the bird that fly freely in the sky,
Without any fear of that one day to die.
Sometimes it's better to be the queen of your own,
Instead of becoming a princess of the fawn.
Love the mistakes that you make,
Not for those who seems to be fake.
Purest of your soul that makes you the whole,
Stay in the mood that keeps you in the stroll.
Find the attachment to keep loving the most,
When you have yourself something to boast.
Be that messy one, whom people feels the crazy one,
Do all the maddest stuff you love,
Which people thinks to be shove.
Love the way you are, not for those who thinks,
Who the hell you are?

98
Shades of Love
Sukrutha TS, Yuvakshetra institute of Management Studies
Palakkad

Then arriving to this globe
Tenderness of that gentle touch
eloquented a mother's love.
Contributing and developing holding his secured hands
Perceived a father's love
Randomly since birth, being together, the affinity of each other
Realised a siblings love
Care at times of trouble and sorrows, exalted with a companions
love.
In a world of changes and chaos, knowing about
the one who was certain enough
found her shoulder to cry on
Discerned the of a better half
Wandering within herself
Sticking to her own companionship
Acquired her self love.

99
Death
Archana PV, University Campus, Calicut

He is dead,
I was under the guava tree we were swinging.
I know him well.
His big face is as ripe as guava fruit
Swinging ropes hanging down from them like a wrinkled body.
While there, he would talk more about his accidental death.
He asks from time to time,
Who are we?
We move unnoticed in front of a camera moved by someone.
We are answering questions of a psychiatrist from another world.

He would look at the empty Bottles in the bar and praise the
courage of the men who would rushed to the house of the dead.

"The first time I felt like dying,
When my girlfriend told me she was not in love
She was the only woman in the world who made me eternal."

He would kiss anyone who feared his long eyes and curly hair.
He even kissed me once.
He learned the language of cats and advises them not to hurt
each other.
He prayed every night that the old woman selling flowers on the
street should not die.
He was afraid of the high hill,
Sea, the speed of the vehicles Why, even the white bed.

During the day people are covered in white blankets and in dark
they meet each other.

The night he died,
I could hear the piano singing from the wings of glitters.

But I know
He still doesn't know, he is dead.

100
Palette of Love
Waheeda Bi Khan, Karnatak University PG Centre
Kodibag, Karnataka

If one tries to paint love
Wonder what hues, its palette hold.
May be-
Some mighty edges of white
Of selfless purity and everlasting bond
For humble devotion and indulgent motherhood.

Amid thick strokes of scarlet
Of intense passions and ardent youth
For sensuous desires and carnal needs.

Few helpless smudges of yellow
Of desperate clinging and fickle moods
For poaching mates and caging obsessions.

Many wonderful spots of pink
Of fresh attractions and tender responses
For innocent wishes and poignant hopes.

Some ugly splotches of mossy green
Of impulsive jealousy and insecure envy
For blind rages and violent suspicions.

Or even clumsy sprays of purple
Of choking tears and snatched smiles
For poisoning words and sliced hearts.

Also few rare sparkles of blue
Of fulfilled dreams and soulful lives
For ageless emotions and transcending affections.

And lo! The canvas it creates
May never cease to baffle and amaze
For love,

May help tame some
While others go berserk;
Can tenderly build a nest
Or destroy empires to doom;
May gush out, even off a rocky-heart
While turn to ice tender spring of other.

The palette of love, so,
Holds all these and more
And stops never, painting itself
In fresh blends and new shades
Till eternity and beyond.